PLENARY REVIEW

PLENARY REVIEW
A MACRO–POLICY APPROACH TO IMPROVE PUBLIC POLICY

BY **DAVID G. WILLIAMS**

A PROJECT OF THE
INTERACTIVITY
FOUNDATION

THINK ABOUT...® PRESS, 1992

Published by Think About . . .® Press for the Interactivity Foundation.

Copyright ©1991 by David Williams and the Interactivity Foundation.
All rights reserved.

Printed in the United States of America.

FIRST EDITION

Book Design by James F. Bennett Jr.
Text set in 11pt. Galliard. Text pages are printed on recycled paper (over 50% deinked recycled paper including 10% from post-consumer sources). This paper exceeds current EPA guidelines for recycled papers.

No part of this book may be used, reproduced or transmitted in any form or by any means whatsoever without the prior written permission of both the copyright owner and the above publisher, except in the case of brief quotations embodied in critical articles or reviews.

Library of Congress Cataloging-in-Publication Data
Williams, David G.
Plenary review : a macro-policy approach to improve public policy / by David G. Williams. – 1st ed.
    p. cm.
Includes bibliographical references.
ISBN 1-879727-02-1 (Hardcover): $24.95
1. Policy Sciences. 2. Political planning–United States.
3. United States–Politics and government–Decision making.
4. United States. Congress. I. Interactivity Foundation (West Virginia) II. Title
H97.W545 1992
320'.6'0973–dc20   92–6604

Think About . . .® Press
364 1/2 Patteson Drive, Suite 257
Morgantown, WV 26505
(800) 835-6294

Invitation to Network

The Interactivity Foundation and the author welcome comments and suggestions of all kinds on Plenary Review and related topics. Interested persons are invited to join the informal network of individuals who discuss Plenary Review and use the concept in various projects. Please contact either of the following:

Dr. David Williams, Chair and Professor
Department of Public Administration
302 Woodburn Hall
West Virginia University
Morgantown, WV 26506

Interactivity Foundation
Post Office Box 8
Parkersburg, WV 26102-0008

To Jay Stern, whose dedication to the public good combines with individual responsibility, whose invigoration of thought combines with patience of development, whose exceptional vision combines with practical action, and whose motivating experience combines with solutions.

CONTENTS

PREFACE	XII
PART I: THE PLENARY REVIEW CONCEPT	17
ONE:	
THE NEED FOR GOVERNANCE LEVEL POLICY REVIEW	19
Policy at the Level of Governance	19
The Exploration of New Ideas	21
The Governance Level Policy Gap	22
Inadequacies in Public Policy Decisions	26
The Need for Periodic Assessment of Consequences	27
The Need for Integrated Coherent Policy	30
The Need for Macro-Policies	32
The Need for Responsive Policy Action	33
The Need for Adaptive Learning	36
The Need for Organic Adaptation	38
The Need for Steering	39
Summary	40

TWO:
THE CORE ELEMENTS OF PLENARY REVIEW — 41
   Assessment of Consequences — 44
   Periodic Review of Public Policy — 48
   Macro-Policy and a Broader Perspective — 50
   More Coherent and Integrated Policy Arenas — 54
   Guiding Direction and Adaptive Action — 56
   The Plenary Review Decision Process — 58
      The Deliberative Process — 58
      Requirement for Decision — 60
      Quantitative Resolution — 61
   Summary: The Plenary Review Mode — 63

THREE:
PLENARY REVIEW CONTRIBUTIONS
TO PUBLIC POLICY DECISIONS — 41
   A Decision Process for Public Bodies — 66
   The Practical Focus of Plenary Review — 67
   The Transforming Influence of Plenary Review — 68
   Plenary Review and Decision Making Rationality — 76
   Interaction of Viewpoints — 81
   Summary — 83

FOUR:
PLENARY REVIEW AS GOVERNANCE — 84
   Concerns for Constitutional Revision — 84
   Concerns for Congressional Reform — 87
   Governance Policy Review — 90
   Plenary Review and Government Control — 93
      Plenary Review as Structural Middle Ground — 94
      Plenary Review Addressing the Balance — 95
      Plenary Review Adds to the Debate — 96
   Governance Action in a Pluralistic Process — 96
   The Risks of Plenary Review — 98
   Plenary Review and the Public Interest — 100
      Traditional Constitutional Assumptions — 100
      Administrative Idealists — 101
      Political Realists — 101
      Assumptions about the Public Interest — 102
   Governance Worthy of Democratic Ideals — 103

FIVE:
EVALUATING THE PLENARY REVIEW CONCEPT   105
   Plenary Review and High Quality Policy Making   106
   Redesign of the Policy Process   112
   Plenary Review and Public Policy   116

PART II: APPLICATIONS OF PLENARY REVIEW   117

SIX:
THE CONDUCT AND OPERATION OF PLENARY REVIEW   119
   Initiation of Plenary Review   120
      Plenary Review as Agenda Setting   121
      Institutionalizing Plenary Review   121
   Definition of the Policy Arena   122
      Periodic Review   124
      Comprehensive Listing of Policies   124
   Timely Decisions   125
   Deliberative Format   126
   The Information Base for Plenary Review   127
      The Stewardship Report   128
      Staff Support and Information   129
      Information From External Sources   130
   Statement of Guiding Direction   130
      Corrective Action   131
      Implementation of the Guiding Direction   132
   How to Conduct a Plenary Review   134

SEVEN:
PLENARY REVIEW HISTORY AND EXPERIMENTS   137
   Background and Stimulus   137
   The Evolution of the Plenary Review Concept   138
   Plenary Review Experiments   140
      Attempting the Rational Decision   141
      Moving Toward a Deliberative Process   142
      The Role of Expert Input   143
      Interaction in Policy Arenas   143
      Plenary Review in Non-Student Groups   144
   Learning by Doing   148

EIGHT:
PLENARY REVIEW APPLICATIONS — **150**

- Types of Plenary Review Applications — 151
- Plenary Review in Legislative and
  Public Policy Bodies — 153
- Plenary Review in Management Applications — 155
  - Public Management Plenary Review — 156
  - Corporate Plenary Review — 160
  - Plenary Review in Non-Profit Organizations — 162
- Citizen Use of Plenary Review — 162
  - Plenary Review in Citizen Forums — 163
  - Plenary Review in the Classroom — 165
- Summary — 168

NINE:
PLENARY REVIEW IN THE UNITED STATES CONGRESS — **169**

- The Hill Needs Help — 169
- Congressional Plenary Review — 170
  - Plenary Review as a Floor Format — 170
  - Plenary Review in Congressional Committees — 174
  - Special Plenary Review Committees — 175
- Staff Supports — 176
- Implementing Devices — 177
- Interactive Plenary Review with the Executive — 179
- A Plenary Review Illustration — 181
- Plenary Review as a Framework for Reform — 183
  - Congress as a Plenary Review Body — 184
  - A Different Role for the Senate — 186
  - Combined Houses for Plenary Review — 187
  - Adding a Plenary Review Body — 188
- Summary — 189

TEN:
ADOPTION OF PLENARY REVIEW IN POLICY BODIES — 191
   Plenary Review as a Developmental Process — 192
   Forces for Plenary Review Establishment — 194
      External Influences for Change — 194
      Support Through Political Processes — 196
      Network of Champions — 197
      Internal Incentives for Change — 199
      The Impact of a Formative Structure and Process — 202
   Strategies for Different Contingencies — 204
   Summary — 206

BIBLIOGRAPHY — 209

INVITATION TO NETWORK — 221

TABLES AND FIGURES
Table 1-1 Hierarchy of Policy Frameworks — 24
Table 1-2 General Policy Reviews — 29
Figure 1-1 Single-Loop and Double-Loop Learning — 37

Table 2-1 Plenary Review Characteristics — 43
Table 2-2 Comparison of Congressional Modes — 43
Table 2-3 Plenary Review Core Elements — 64
Table 2-4 Plenary Review Process Elements — 65

Table 3-1 Influence of the Assessment of Consequences — 69
Table 3-2 Influence of Periodic Review — 70
Table 3-3 Influence of Macro-Policy and Broader Perspective — 71
Table 3-4 Influence of More Integrated and Cohesive Policy — 72
Table 3-5 Influence of the Guiding Direction — 73
Table 3-6 Influence of a Deliberative Process — 74
Table 3-7 Influence of Requirement for Decision — 75
Table 3-8 Influence of Quantitative Resolution — 76

Table 4-1 Plenary Review and Governance	92
Table 5-1 Requisites of High Quality Policy Making	107
Table 5-2 Plenary Review and High Quality Policy Making	111
Table 5-3 Principles and Strategies for Policy Making Redesign	112
Table 5-4 Plenary Review and Change in the Policy System	115
Table 6-1 How to Conduct a Plenary Review	134
Table 6-2 An Overview of Plenary Review	136
Table 7-1 Plenary Review Development	145
Table 8-1 General Plenary Review Types	152
Table 8-2 Degrees of Plenary Review Application	153
Table 8-3 Plenary Review in a City Council	155
Table 8-4 Plenary Review in Public Agencies	158
Table 8-5 Plenary Review in Private Corporations	161
Table 8-6 Plenary Review in a Citizen Forum	164
Table 8-7 Plenary Review in the Classroom	167
Table 9-1 Plenary Review in Congress	173
Table 10-1 Force for Adoption: External Influences	196
Table 10-2 Force for Adoption: Development of Political Support	197
Table 10-3 Force for Adoption: Network of Champions	198
Table 10-4 Plenary Review and Legislative Incentives	200

PREFACE

There are few challenges greater than designing and implementing effective public policy and thereby achieving the public good. This book identifies some critical needs and then proposes a major redesign of the policy-making system to meet those needs. Such an exercise treads on difficult territory, but significant questions often require exploration of promising concepts.

A word or two about the origin of the topic and the proposed improvement—Plenary Review—is appropriate here (more background is provided in Chapter Seven). Julius (Jay) Stern fathered and has helped to rear the concept of Plenary Review in an interesting combination of the practical and the conceptual. Many academics write insightfully in various areas of public policy, and many have even served in various responsible governmental positions implementing such policy; but few have been at the conjunction of policy practice and concept such as has been the experience of Jay Stern. Stern, a Parkersburg, West Virginia, businessman, has long had interest in questions of philosophy and public policy. A lifetime of thought and reading and practical experience in public policies (particularly relating

Preface

XIII

to banking and the environment) have given him insight into some crucial public policy issues. In the matters dealing with the Clean Air Act, Stern Bros., Inc., has been an important facilitator establishing a middle ground. In public policy relating to banking, a stand on moral principle led to the voluntary deeding of a bank to reduce the national debt rather than compromise that principle. In short, the experience and thought of Jay Stern have animated and continue to animate the proposal of Plenary Review as an attempt to meet some important practical and conceptual public policy needs.

Since this study is somewhat unusual, a few comments concerning its approach may prove helpful. The investigation of a new idea requires an approach which is developmental and conceptual, but which is anchored in practical application. The study proposes ways and means by which governmental actors may begin to address basic challenges to our polity. It deals with the basic concerns of effective governance. The author is mindful that this will raise a host of fundamental analytic issues which have concerned scholars and policy makers alike for generations.

The main focus of this book is the development of a concept of policy review—Plenary Review. Plenary Review is proposed to initiate public consideration and debate of this promising concept. Most academic studies attempt to understand what is; this study directs creative thought to what ought to be. Readers may differ with the recommendations presented here; regardless, the study attempts to grapple with some of our government's most intractable problems. As Nelson Polsby observed in *Political Innovation in America*, even when leaders see problems and even when there are built-in incentives, "the actual solutions must come from somewhere" (1984: 1-65). Plenary Review is presented as one concept for meeting some policy needs.

In many respects, this book is an exercise in political engineering. This study is not simply analytical, it is avowedly prescriptive; it offers various proposals to meet the needs identified through analysis. Such an approach is in the tradition of the Founders of the nation. Austin Ranney, in his presidential address to the American Political Science Association, noted that American political science arose out of the heritage of "political engineering" and what was called the "divine science of politics" (1976: 144-147). This faith, that there are solutions and that it is better to do something even if less than perfect, has animated many movements in the American experience (such as the direct primary and the New Deal). Ranney called for political engineering directed to pressing problems. He recognized that many in political science would disagree about whether the discipline should (or can) develop knowledge immediately useful for the solution of practical social problems. But he left no question about his view when he said:

> What place can we honestly give *today* to our traditional faith in political engineering? I, for one, feel that faith still merits a judgement once made by a wise man about the process of growing old: "It's not for sissies," he said, "but it beats the alternative." If the alternative in this case is the resigned acceptance of human impotence and passivity in the face of human misery, then surely political engineering, with all its faults and failures, beats that. (Ranney, 1976: 147-148.)

A brief note on the organization of the book may be helpful. The chapters in Part I identify important needs in the public policy system and present Plenary Review as a way to meet those needs. While the chapters in Part I present and evaluate the Plenary Review concept, the chapters in Part II discuss possible applications and uses of Plenary Review. Of necessity, the chapters in Part II will be more developmental and experimental in applying Plenary Review to a wide range of public policy bodies.

Any book is the result of efforts by many who are not identified on the title page. The author is most grateful to both Jay Stern and the Interactivity Foundation for their generous financial and intellectual support of the experimental, research and sabbatical projects leading to this book. The concept of Plenary Review is one which the Interactivity Foundation has pursued in a variety of projects and efforts. This book is one effort in the Foundation's continuing concern and work in Plenary Review and other project areas. The Foundation and the author welcome comments and suggestions on Plenary Review and related topics. Interested readers are invited to join the informal network of individuals who discuss Plenary Review and use the concept in various projects. The Interactivity Foundation and the author may be contacted at the addresses given on the verso of the title page.

A good many of the concepts and phrases in this book are not my own. Beyond those referenced in traditional academic fashion are the ideas which have developed out of Plenary Review discussions for more than six years. Discussions with Jay Stern and scores of others have produced insights and ideas which are so intermixed as to make unnecessary the designation of the originator. Many concepts went

PREFACE

through growth in the best tradition of brainstorming where one has a glimmer of an idea, another adds to it and ideas are developed. In many ways, my function in this book has been as recorder and contributor rather than author and owner of all ideas presented here. Much is owed to the core individuals who have contributed to these many discussions and projects. In addition to Jay Stern, Joseph Albright has contributed many insights, particularly from his experience as Speaker of the House of Delegates in West Virginia. David Webber, University of Missouri, contributed his thoughts, efforts and suggestions over many years. Max Stephenson, Virginia Polytechnic Institute and State University, has been a great help in both concept and style. Gerald Pops, West Virginia University, has been supportive at critical points. Many other scholars and practitioners, as well as hundreds of participants in the various projects, receive grateful thanks. As always, limitations of concept and presentation remain my responsibility. A last note of acknowledgement and support are due my wife, Mary, and our four daughters, Cara, Amy, Jan and Angela.

David G. Williams
Morgantown, West Virginia
Spring, 1992

PART I:
THE PLENARY REVIEW CONCEPT

Our current policy systems are generally unable to provide an adequate sense of purpose or to instill a common vision. Chapter One identifies inadequacies in the policy system. Chapter Two then presents Plenary Review as an approach to meet these important needs.

Chapter Three discusses how Plenary Review contributes to and influences policy decisions made by public bodies. Chapter Four notes concerns with effective governance, specifically with respect to the effectiveness of Congress and the constitutional system. Plenary Review is discussed as a governance level mode to deal with these concerns. The final chapter in Part I, Chapter Five, evaluates the Plenary Review concept with regard to high quality policy making and the policy process.

Chapters in Part I will present the Plenary Review concept. Issues of operation and application will be developed in Part II.

ONE: THE NEED FOR GOVERNANCE LEVEL POLICY REVIEW

Plenary Review is a bold idea for improving governance and public policy. This is a time when the makers of public policy and the public alike share an abiding concern for more effective public policy. There is great dissatisfaction with legislative actions and executive leadership. Both opinion leaders and citizens are severely critical of a wide range of policies and programs and of governmental effectiveness in general. This book argues that elements critical to policy effectiveness are either missing or poorly performed. Plenary Review is proposed as a means to achieve more effective governance and better pursue the public interest in decisions on public policies and programs.

POLICY AT THE LEVEL OF GOVERNANCE

This chapter evaluates public policy making at the level of governance. It describes some of the important deficiencies and inadequacies which following chapters will attempt to remedy. The challenging task at hand is to develop a public policy mode useful at a higher level of generality than programs and specific policies, to convert the power and authority of governments into more effective normative instruments and thus to make government ultimately more effective (see Meehan, 1990: 201). There needs to be something above our current policy systems which will create better understanding, enable assessment of the consequences of past actions, assist the development of directions and purposes, and inform policy details and actions.

This discussion must take us beyond current policy approaches and debates. The larger questions need to be asked and deliberated. It is not just a matter of improving current processes, improving research, adding staff and fine-tuning methods. For example, even if Congress were to excel in the ability to handle their routine legislative responsibilities—and this would be a major advance—we still need to ask whether the routine should be done at all, where it is taking us, what the consequences of past decisions are, and where we should be going. The major challenge is not just to improve the operational efficiency of Congress or other policy bodies; rather, the major mission is conceptual—to think about destiny, trends and vision and to give guiding direction.

Of course, it is important that our public institutions are well led and well managed. However, it makes little sense to be diligently climbing the ladder of good policy development and implementation only to find that the ladder may be against the wrong wall. And we have many public institutions that are over-managed at the same time they are under-led (Bennis, 1989). Since it is important to be well led, this book focuses at a higher level of generality than most policy approaches to ask these larger questions.

The focus in this chapter and in the presentation of Plenary Review is governance level policy review. Rather than focus on whether we are doing things right, we need to focus on whether we are doing the right thing. We must take the long view, rather than the short view. We need to understand what and why, not just how. We must be oriented to the future while based on the past, rather than just trying to improve the present. We need to focus on direction and tone, not just program and policy specifics. We seek vision, not just operational effectiveness. We must think in terms of development and responsiveness, rather than efficiency and maintenance (adapted from Bennis, 1989: 77).

The Exploration of New Ideas

One understandable reaction to governance level policy review is that it is utopian and unrealistic. While there is some substance to this point, readers are invited to consider fully the important concepts in the following chapters.

Jean Jacques Rousseau once suggested, "There is nothing more difficult to take in hand, more perilous to conduct, or more uncertain in its success than to take the lead in the introduction of a new order of things." This book presents a bold but nascent idea—Plenary Review—which can ultimately have a significant impact. In considering a grand idea, the reader will have to confront significant issues and oftentimes remote possibilities. Such an effort is buoyed by the hope offered by Ortega y Gasset:

> "Man has been able to grow enthusiastic over his vision of . . . unconvincing enterprises. He has put himself to work for the sake of an idea, seeking by magnificent exertions to arrive at the incredible. And in the end, he has arrived there. Beyond all doubt it is one of the vital sources of man's power, to be thus able to kindle enthusiasm from the mere glimmer of something improbable, difficult, remote."
> (1966: 1)

Nelson Polsby has professed value in those who "think deeply about problems, who search for and invent alternatives—inventors, adaptors, policy entrepreneurs, brokers, incubators" (1984: 174). He has contended that "it is on the energy and ingenuity of just such persons that the capacity of a complex society to adapt and meet new needs depends. And upon them also not infrequently rests the task of creating the indispensable substance that the political process processes." Plenary Review is presented in this spirit as an idea worthy of widespread consideration.

Attempts to propose significant improvements—such as Plenary Review—are not unknown or unsuccessful in our system. Indeed, the creation of the Constitution itself provides an excellent referent. It was the result of highly self-conscious efforts in the constitutional convention to apply to particular situations principles which had been debated and developed. This was political engineering at its best;

John Adams spoke of the "divine science of politics" (Ranney, 1976: 141-142). It was a lofty attempt to design significant improvements in the governance system. Plenary Review does not reach so far, yet it suggests some important revisions in the decision processes used to enact public policies.

Given the task at hand, the approach or methodology in this chapter is conceptual rather than empirical. Concepts, particularly ones which are innovative or out of the line of traditional discourse, are often poorly perceived and evaluated through traditional definitions and frameworks because these are often inadequate to provide the potentially richer understanding inherent in the notion. This Chapter illustrates the need for Plenary Review through the use of observations and metaphors. This will provide a richer understanding of Plenary Review and the needs it is designed to meet. The reader will sense the truth of these assertions about the policy system and the challenges to governance.

The redirecting of thought is usually necessary for full consideration of innovative notions. Gareth Morgan has suggested that "since problems may be a natural consequence of the logic of the system in which they are found, we may be able to deal with the problems only by restructuring the logic" (1986: 270). He has contended that "we can overcome many familiar problems by learning to see and understand . . . in new ways so that new courses of action emerge" (1986: 336). Harlan Cleveland has observed that we are conditioned by past history to see policy-making and governance in certain ways; our perceptions and actions are guided by this history (1988). The new perspective will lay the foundation for Plenary Review by describing a governance level policy gap, critical inadequacies in our current policy approaches, and the need for better systemic adaptive learning.

THE GOVERNANCE LEVEL POLICY GAP

There is a need for policy thinking at a higher level of generality than found in most policy bodies, particularly legislatures. This higher level of generality is sometimes called macro-policy or meta-policy, but it is well described by discussing a gap in our levels of policy. Macro-policy is understood as general principles, purposes and norms which guide the making of public policy. Macro-policy provides a framework so that legislation and other policy enactments can form a more coherent whole and so that executive actions and administrative rules and regulations can be guided in their implementing interpretations. Above the level of statutory enactment and other policy statements are questions of desired ends, beliefs and values which generate policy and which describe the ends to which policy is the means. Macro-policy may be conceived of as the underlying justification and the positive guidance for policy actions.

Yehezkel Dror sketched four levels of policy response: the micro-response level (particular policies), the mezzo-response level (medium or short-term reactions), the macro-response level (dealing with general policy areas), and the social-process level (grand developmental trends such as attempted by Toynbee and Spengler) (1986: 47-51). In this terminology, Plenary Review might be classified as macro-response policy with occasional excursions into the social-process level. Plenary Review is an attempt to conceive, evaluate and act beyond particular or short-term policy actions.

Given this description of macro-policy, where is the gap? The hierarchy of governance directives for our national government ranges from the Constitution, statutory legislation, executive orders, rules and regulations to implementing administrative orders (also relevant are judicial findings and attorney general interpretations). These may be seen as frameworks at successively specific levels. As illustrated below, there is a gap between the Constitution and statutory frameworks. Plenary Review will be proposed to provide a macro-policy framework (of guiding purposes) between statutory enactment and constitutional provision.

There are different levels of policy language and different degrees of specificity in that language. Specificity of view and language is greatest at the direct program operating level, more general at the agency middle-management level, broader still at the agency policy level, most general at the level of presidential policy and legislative enactments (although many statutes and presidential orders also include detailed provisions). Then, a gap may be discerned between these and the constitutional level. The Constitution gives general shape to the governance system, but it does not itself address many important policy concerns, substantive questions, larger philosophical issues and the assessment of consequences and ends. Of course, it was not intended that the Constitution would address all these issues. The Constitution provides the governance system and institutional framework within which these questions can be addressed.

TABLE 1-1
HIERARCHY OF POLICY FRAMEWORKS

Level	Products
Constitutional Law	General purposes, structure, and processes
Governance Level Policy Gap	Guiding directions, purposes, substantive goals, policy principles
Statutory Law	Programs and policies
Administrative Law	Executive orders, rules and regulations
Implementing Direction	Policy procedures, manuals, operating instructions and interpretations

Since there is no guiding framework which relates constitutional provisions to macro-policy concerns, the governance system has had to interpret constitutional provisions through legislative, judicial and executive actions. This, of course, is proper and necessary; however, it is often done indirectly and through narrow issues. The courts have played a major role in interpreting policy at all levels including the macro-policy level. In some respects, the Court has had to act to fill some gaps in the absence of more-detailed constitutional provision or legislative action. In fact, this role for the Supreme Court was not explicitly envisioned by all Founders or assigned in the Constitution, but had, itself, to be judicially interpreted. In many areas, it is primarily through interpretation and what Price calls the "unwritten constitution" of practices and procedures that the Constitution is applicable to today (1983: 8). If we are to maintain an effective constitutional framework, then the processes (such as Plenary Review) which will enable adaptation and updating are important to consider. (The capacity of Congress to accomplish such a review is an important question which will be treated in a later chapter.)

This is an important issue; it is important to have an effective constitutional framework for effective governance. Weakness in the constitutional system can render a government ineffective, devitalized and unable to govern effectively (Sundquist, 1986: 4-12). The necessity for an effective constitutional framework does not require a revised constitution if there is adequate provision for renewal and currency and for meeting general policy principles and purposes.

There has been increasing attention to the problems of governance. A recent book from the Brookings Institution is entitled *Can Government Govern?* The book argued that "the problems of governance in the United States is mainly one of creating institutions or governing arrangements that can pursue policies of sufficient coherence, consistency, foresight, and stability that the national welfare is not sacrificed for narrow or temporary gains" (Chubb and Peterson, 1989, p. 4).

Charles O. Jones discussed a similar notion in his evaluation of the congressional policy process: "Reaching conclusions is a more comprehensive process than simply passing laws" (1975: 269). Decisions must include the broad range of defining problems, setting priorities, determining policy and overseeing implementation. He argued that democracy is threatened when this is not done well by Congress. He quoted Theodore Lowi to the effect that we get "policy without law" (Jones, 1975: 269). In *America's Unwritten Constitution*, Don Price contended that Congress was too frequently preoccupied with the niggling details of policy implementation. He argued that the orientation to the details of administration was widespread and dysfunctional. He urged an array of changes designed to focus congressional attention on the "big picture" of policy making (Price, 1983; see Stillman, 1988: 815). There is a need to focus on the overarching rationale, the macro-policy, which gives vision and legitimacy to particular policy actions at a grander level than legislation, but within the constitutional framework.

Plenary Review calls for a larger congressional role in establishing guiding macro-policies. Since both the Supreme Court and the Congress have limitations and strengths in this interpretive role, an active role for each may complement the other. At a minimum, greater legislative concern for macro-policy matters can improve legislative perspective and effectiveness and can enhance updating and adaptation without requiring constitutional revision.. The central point is simply that consideration should be given to innovative approaches which would more effectively deal with the larger issues of constitutional development and macro-policy.

This discussion has used the federal level to illustrate the need for macro-policy and for directing attention to the policy gap. The gap, however, is common to most public policy bodies. Most policy bodies need to debate and determine macro-policy. In so doing, they confront the general principles and ends of policies, inform both policy deliberation and implementation, and guide future policy and its outcomes. The public policy decision process is enhanced by the macro-policy perspective in policy bodies at all levels.

INADEQUACIES IN PUBLIC POLICY DECISIONS

This section will argue that there are critical inadequacies in the decision approaches used by most bodies to debate and decide public policy. At the same time, there are tremendous challenges to be met. The heart of the matter is the inability of legislatures, policy bodies and governing boards to deal with what could be called "wicked" problems. Rittel and Webber have argued that there are two basic types of policy issues: "tame" problems and "wicked" problems (1973: 160). Tame policy problems, such as paving roads, lend themselves well to solutions arising from common sense and professional expertise. Wicked policy problems, however, evidence no ready solutions and are typically characterized by temporary and imperfect resolutions. Wicked problems usually enjoy no definitive formulation and no commonly accepted evaluative criteria. Instead, wicked issues are the target of numerous political definitions, and proposed solutions become part of the continuing discussion of policy problems. There is a steadily growing need for increased effectiveness in dealing with wicked problems.

Our governmental bodies have not been very successful in dealing with wicked problems. The regulation of savings and loans, banks and other financial institutions is a good case in point. The savings and loan mess is as much a public policy crisis as a financial crisis. The deficit and budget debates, particularly those of 1990, are another example of wicked problems. Indeed, almost any group— from seminars to cocktail parties—can readily come up with a list of public policy areas where there are grave problems.

The challenges facing effective decisions on public policy may well become even more critical. In *Policymaking Under Adversity* (1986), Yehezkel Dror surveyed about thirty countries to review policy challenges and attempts in each to meet these. He concluded that "policy adversity seems to be epochal, with a high probability of getting worse during the next thirty-year span and beyond" (1986: 44, 60). The main predicaments confronting public policy, in his view, are shifts in policy issues, erosion of the political base and absence of reliable policy compasses (Dror, 1986: 23-35). He also noted difficulties stemming from diminished trust, fragmentation of political resources, elimination of transcendental justifications and reduced monopoly of compliance. Since adversities pose challenges beyond the capacity of present policy-making systems, Dror concluded that attempts to improve policy-making systems "emerge as one of the better bets in human endeavors to influence futures in desired directions through collective deliberate interventions" (1986: 241).

The difficulties which confront effective governance and policy making are complex and intractable—"wicked." Although there are many concerns about our policy systems, there are four central inadequacies toward which Plenary Review is directed. The first concern is that the social, moral, political, economic and institutional consequences of public policies are not adequately assessed on a periodic basis. The second is that public policies are inadequately reviewed to identify interrelationships and establish coherent integrated policy. The third concern is that general public purposes and guiding macro-policies are inadequately determined. The fourth concern is that there is inadequate policy leadership, periodic adjustment and responsiveness. These points question whether public policy decision processes and the policies which result are adequate to meet the challenges being confronted, whether there is adequate understanding of the changing context and whether the authority and legitimacy of public bodies and their policies may be undermined. These four inadequacies will be discussed in the following sections.

The Need for Periodic Assessment of Consequences

There is a need in public policy decisions to assess more effectively the consequences of public policy on a periodic basis. An effective review process would include the long-range view and a deliberative assessment of important consequences. And, to be effective, these must be done periodically. What, for example, might successive public policies on tobacco and smoking or on banking have been if in each of the last ten decades there had been an assessment of consequences and adjustment of policy?

The need for a long-range perspective stems from the need in today's world for forethought, preparation, anticipation and planning. Even basic issues and needs change over time. The resolution of old issues and the continuance of old compromises may make little sense in new contexts and changing times. The old rationales do not necessarily fit new situations. The long-range view is needed to enable policy-makers to develop and act on new rationales. This is a challenge for the Congress, the executive and most other policy bodies. For example, congressional review of important public policy—such as health care, housing or welfare—is now largely limited to short-term policies and programs. Legislatures and other policy bodies have everywhere been impelled by particular and parochial interests, rather than being directed toward the needs of the jurisdiction as a whole. Public policy decisions will benefit from focusing on the larger and more global issues (Cleveland, 1988: 684-685).

Not only is the long-range perspective needed, it is important to review policy arenas in terms of their impact and consequences. Specifically, what are the moral, economic, political, social and institutional consequences of a policy? When these are not fully recognized and debated, policy action can too easily have a mistaken focus and ineffective results. An assessment of consequences bases judgement on actual experience. This orientation would strengthen the ability of public policy bodies to meet changes with intelligent anticipation. Without resolving the debate about democratic planning (for example, Tugwell argues that democracy may not survive without it [1970: ix], while Friedman argues that it is incompatible with democracy [1988: 130-135]), intelligent forethought is likely to be more effective than its absence.

The decision approach which understands consequences and takes the long-range view also enables learning. An ability to assess what is happening and to take action, make some mistakes, institute corrections and take a broad view—to learn as the system operates—is very important to policy effectiveness. This critical point will be further developed later in the chapter through the metaphors of adaptive learning, organism and steering. This does not mean that all decisions must be right, but rather that they add to the process of insight and understanding. "Learning by doing" is a phrase that encapsulates much wisdom for ongoing development of public policy.

The need for the long-range view and the assessment of consequences directs attention to a related need—that of periodic review. Many policies, once established, are rarely revisited. There is a great need to review the consequences regularly in major policy arenas to identify if the outcomes are severally beneficial, no longer desired or adverse to preferred ends. As policies and programs accumulate rules, regulations, amendments, interpretations and practices in their implementation, they often change radically. In addition, contexts and conditions change. It thus becomes critical for public bodies to periodically review major policies.

Is such a periodic review of public policy needed? Many groups seem to think so as judged by the number of such attempts stimulated by the turn of the decade and the policy challenges of the 1990s. Table 1-2 lists many of these efforts.

TABLE 1-2
GENERAL POLICY REVIEWS

Organization	Book	Citation
Urban Institute	*Challenge to Leadership: Economic and Social Issues for the Next Decade*	Sawhill, 1988
Heritage Foundation	*Mandate for Leadership III: Policy Strategies for the 1990s*	Heatherly and Pines, 1989
Hoover Institution	*Thinking About America: The United States in the 1990s*	Anderson and Bark, 1988
Democracy Project	*America's Transition: Blueprints for the 1990s*	Green and Pinsky, 1989
Center for National Policy	*America Tomorrow: The Choices We Face*	Steinbruner, 1989
Committee on the Constitutional System	*Government for the Third American Century*	Robinson, 1989
Institute of Cultural Conservatism	*Cultural Conservatism: Toward a New National Agenda*	Institute, 1988
Joint Center for Political Studies	*Black Economic Progress: An Agenda for the 1990s*	Simms, 1989
Ripon Society	*A Newer World: The Progressive Republican Vision of America*	Leach and McKenzie, 1988

In summary, the decision processes for most public policies inadequately assess the moral, social, economic, political and institutional consequences on a periodic basis. This long-range view is important to effective decisions and effective public policy. Of course, most policy bodies—the Congress included—take long-range views and assess consequences, but these actions are rarely focused and sufficient to meet the policy challenges. Plenary Review will be presented as one approach to better meet these needs.

The Need for Integrated Coherent Policy

Are the policy decision processes in Congress adequate to meet the need for integrated, coherent policy? Many well-informed persons do not think so. Alice Rivlin, based on her experience heading the Congressional Budget Office, argued that Congress would be doing its job more effectively if it "concentrated on major policy issues rather than on details of program management" (1987: 7). Senator Bill Brock has commented that the Senate gets into day-to-day debates "without a national or broad perspective, without an overview, or foresight capacity" (Sundquist, 1981: 417). Sundquist has contended that one important missing capability of Congress is Congress as policy integrator (1981: 427-439). He commented further that the activities of government must be in support of the objectives, they must be in balance, and there must be a sense of the totality. Don Price has observed that Congress does not do well in establishing a comprehensive view, forging difficult compromises or pushing through enactment (Price, 1985: 163-165). Davidson and Oleszek have observed that policy-making resembles a "meat slicer, reducing large public problems to a series of discrete, unrelated and often contradictory tidbits of policy" (1977: x). Kingdon described the system of policy fragmentation as the right and left hands not knowing each other's actions, the consequences of which are disjointed policy, lack of common concern and agenda instability (1984: 124-138, 151).

A critical need in many areas of public policy is for consistency. Some policies fight lung cancer and discourage smoking while other policies subsidize tobacco. Responses to policy challenges are inadequate without integration. Various modes of transportation have various policies which are not interrelated in any cohesive transportation policy. Policy exists, of course, in most areas, but it is often fragmented, confusing and not correlated with interdependent policies.

The general need for integrated coherent policy can be illustrated by an additional example. The public policy enactments and their interpreting implementation which guide the banking system in the

United States need to have a broad review. There have been many developments in banking which have resulted in major modifications. Congress has neither designed these by formal action nor has it fully reviewed their consequences and impact. A broad review of public policy in banking would need to address the impact of banking deregulation, the conditions of a competitive market, the consequences of monetary policy, the influence of consumer capital needs, the types of desired competition and the design of the deposit insurance system, to name just a few issues. The review should note the consequences of banking public policy and practice from moral, social, political, economic and institutional points of view and design appropriate action based on those judgements. Congress has initiated a belated review of banking in 1991, however, the scope is limited and the timing follows rather than anticipates major crises.

The absence of coherent policy is illustrated in further examples. In transportation, for example, *The Economist* reported that Sam Skinner, the Secretary of the Department of Transportation, is "preparing to step gingerly into this mess. For the first time in the country's history, he will be presenting a national transport policy" (*Economist*: 7-14-89). In another area, Herbert Stein reviewed the American economy and its relation to investment, education, care of the very poor and defense and concluded that "the decision-making process is inadequate" (Stein, 1989: 8). An article in the *Wall Street Journal* was entitled "Doing Badly Trying to Do Good on Capitol Hill." The first sentence recognized the problems of coherence when it stated that "Congress, as it weaves ever more complex legislative webs, displays less and less capacity to manage its responsibilities" (Melloan, 1989). The need for integrated and coherent policy is easily illustrated in Congress, but it is also a genuine need in many other policy bodies.

Nor are the limitations of congressional policy-making fully remedied by the actions of the other branches. While the President does have a national constituency, and can propose an integrated policy program, the President has not always provided consistent and coherent policy direction. The policy responsibility of the judicial branch has been limited by design. Its policy function is largely interpretive, retrospective, and specifically applicable to the individuals involved. It is based on constitutional and statutory grounds rather than on the anticipation of developing needs. It is essentially passive until a case is brought before the court (Eidelberg, 1974: 159-160, 168-169).

Incremental and piece-meal actions, never attempting the broad view or searching for coherence, are largely ineffective in anticipating and handling major challenges. Without the broad policy view, one is never certain where to go, why one should go, and, indeed, if one ever moves in that direction. Fragmented, incremental policy will not provide the vision and leadership to meet rising needs. The policy decision system in many bodies is often inadequate to identify the important interrelationships and interdependence of policies and to establish coherent integrated policy.

The Need for Macro-Policies

While there should not and can not be agreement and guidance on everything, policy decisions are strengthened by consideration of central public purposes—macro-policy. A surer sense of "what we are" and "where we want to go" need to guide governance actions, provide criteria to assess performance and invigorate action. All the right answers or purposes are not ascertainable, but the processes of debate, analysis, political interplay, voting, and so forth may be as important as the goal. In bodies establishing public policy, there needs to be debate of critical questions, search for answers and establishment of general guidance.

Diversity will continue to stimulate the thought and discussion which contribute so greatly to governance decisions. Macro-policy will always be controversial. Although Barber noted that one of the strengths of the United States has been the *absence* of enduring public purposes (because it has enabled compromises which have permitted the system to flourish, 1979: 20), he has argued that there is now perhaps a current need to better determine public purposes. The point here is simply that an attempt at macro-policy—a concern with ultimate purposes and practical consequences—will produce some benefits.

Effective public policy ultimately undergirds the authority and the legitimacy of the governance system and its decisions. This is a serious concern. Brodkin reported that there has been deterioration in the way political processes and institutions have aggregated and resolved interests, and that under these circumstances policy institutions are unable to provide coherent and consistent policy direction. She contended that government is having difficulty in sustaining its legitimacy because "its political institutions can not manage policy conflict and its bureaucratic institutions can not deliver on policy promises"

(1987: 574-575). Alice Rivlin, who had extended experience with the three branches of government as head of the Congressional Budget Office, reported that the policy system is so complex, diffused and fragmented that it is unable to take effective action (1987: 6-10). She argued that the politics of organization have superseded the politics of ideology, so that the very institutions of governance have become a critical issue.

Public acceptance of governance actions does indeed appear to be a problem. Lipset and Schneider reviewed a long series of public opinion polls and observed a trend of declining trust in government (1983: 29). They did note, however, that the diminishing degree of confidence appears to be more closely linked to the perceived performance of government programs and the behavior of public officials, rather than to the system itself or the norms associated with it.

The comments on legitimacy and effective governance are presented here to illustrate the need for decisions on public policy to consider the important macro-policy issues. The point is simply to establish that there are many important macro-policy issues; Plenary Review will then be presented in the following chapters as one device to address these issues. Broadly described, effective governance depends on doing the right things (guiding toward desired ends), doing things right (managing day-to-day operations) and insuring that right things are done (assessing consequences). Macro-policy is the first element of this triad. Plenary Review is intended to advance the ability of our public policy institutions to deal with these concerns of macro-policy and to navigate better the polity.

The Need for Responsive Policy Action

The energy crisis of the 1970's led to many calls for a national energy policy. However, the Iraqi invasion of Kuwait in the 1990's found the U.S. still without an effective energy policy. Unfortunately, this is the case in many important policy areas. The American system is often known for its ability to stymie and slow policy action rather than for positive policy leadership. Some have even noted a history of distrust of "responsible" policy-making (Price, 1983: 129). Active policy leadership should include both determination of desirable prospective action and direction of adaptive efforts toward their achievement. Toft uses the phrase "civic entrepreneurship" (Toft, 1986: 248-252) to describe prospective policy leadership and adaptive action through strategic thinking, macro-policy deliberation, aggregating support and identifying priorities. There is a critical need for such responsible policy leadership.

The system created by the Constitution clearly has tendencies toward policy incoherence and toward inaction as a result of the fragmentation from checks and balances. This can cause a "deadlock of democracy" and "policy paralysis." Sundquist has argued that the constitutional system leads to stalemate and gridlock and that the congressional incapacities to act quickly and to plan have resulted in the decline and weakness of Congress (1981: 8-9, 155-162). Dodd has noted "policy immobilism" arising out of the separation of powers and congressional weakness (1985: 517). Brodkin pointed to serious limitations in congressional policy-making capacity because of structural and political fragmentation, control by subcommittees and the wide variety of parochial interests (1987: 573). Price has argued that decentralization, particularism and institutionalized fragmentation have stultified congressional effectiveness (1985: 162-163). Rieselbach, a long-time student of Congress, concluded that Congress, as an institution, has not distinguished itself in its performance (1977: 6). In the last four decades, he continued, Congress has too often been found on the side of caution rather than of action. While some call for congressional and constitutional reform, Hamilton argued that the central challenge is to develop policy leadership which can provide a vision and rationale for future adaptation and developments (Hamilton, 1978: 122).

Indeed, the argument can be presented that no one sufficiently governs because the institutions of governance are both too weak to manage a modern political economy and too porous to restrict the demands made upon them (Brodkin, 1987: 571). In the view of the Brookings Institution, the management of "crucial contemporary problems has been disappointing for so many years" that an analytical volume was prompted with the title *Can The Government Govern?* (Chubb and Peterson, 1989). Hugh Heclo noted the implication from the recent emergence of issue networks for the democratic conception of policies determined in the legislative body. He commented on the great danger that issue politics and policy experts would reduce rather than enhance both congressional governance and the protection of liberty and popular government (1978: 121). This might create the strange result of more expert policy participants and their issue networks producing less effective governance.

The Need for Policy Review

It is true, as Dye notes, that policy is both what Congress chooses to do and chooses not to do. Taking no action is also a policy choice. The arguments presented here should not be taken to mean that Congress must always act on everything to establish policy. Rather, the point is that *de facto* policy should not be the result of unawareness, inability or incapacity. There needs to be an awareness and an ability to act or not act, as may be appropriate.

Responsive action is a major governance challenge. Achieving change in limited policy arenas and programs is often difficult enough, but achieving needed change in entrenched institutions and practices is especially daunting. Inability to change easily should be expected, particularly because our current system of governance is large and complex, with a high degree of interdependence among its parts. In addition, there are challenges of inertia in the face of an unknown future. Since change is often resisted even when it is demonstrably good for actors and institutions (Garner, 1988: 1-2), some proactive device is needed to meet needs before circumstances force the change. While crisis may be the mid-wife of change, solutions born of catastrophe may not be the best method of achieving change. If change is left to crisis, the immediate problems overwhelmingly control thought and action. It usually is more advantageous to provide a strategy for oncoming change than be driven by circumstances. This requires some mode (such as Plenary Review) to enable better decision and action.

As Toft has argued, longer-term survival and growth of the polity requires "movement away from a passive/reactive mode to a more proactive mode" (1986: 242). And as George Graham noted in *America's Capacity to Govern* (1960: 84-85), creativity is a critical element in governance leadership. Creativity is directly linked to an ability to recognize societal needs, a compulsion to act in response to perceived needs, a receptivity to new ideas, the power to set goals and the ability to integrate ideas and programs into a whole. The capacity to govern effectively thus can be critically dependent upon creativity and the disposition for leadership action. Of course, some current policy decision processes are concerned with action and innovation. The argument here is that these concerns are insufficiently addressed in most public policy bodies. The need for responsive action has generally not been met. Nor will additional effort alone necessarily be adequate to meet the need.

Given the challenges of change facing public policy, what are the various actions which can be taken? In his book, Dror reviewed various response patterns to policy making under adversity (1986: 51-60). In such circumstances, policy responses may merely reflect coming to terms with adversity in policy making through denial, simplification, externalization, rationalization, reduction of expectations and self-blame. Rather than a challenge, adversity itself can even be perceived as ennobling and purifying. Efforts to avoid rather than meet the problems can be tempting. Action taken may be only nominal or for the sake of appearance. Thinking may be only incremental, with sporadic jumps, rather than thinking in the order and the magnitude appropriate to the challenge. Such responses cope with policy problems in their particular political contexts. They most often are not effective in getting to the core of public policy concerns. Other possible responses to policy making under adversity include great administrative reforms, renewed or new policy "theologies" (guides for action) and grand-policy innovations (1986: 51-60). Another option can be added to Dror's list. Plenary Review will be presented as an action response to governance and policy challenges.

THE NEED FOR ADAPTIVE LEARNING

There is a critical need for adaptive learning in the policies of the American polity at all levels. This need is well described by considering related metaphors such as double-loop learning, learning to learn, social learning, organic adaptation and steering. These each illustrate important capacities critical to effective governance, but which are often not considered when enmeshed in individual policies and program details.

Argyris and Schon distinguished between single-loop and double-loop learning (Argyris, 1982; Argyris & Schon, 1978). Single-loop learning is the ability to detect and correct in relation to a given set of operating norms. The single-loop is the cyclical process of 1) sensing the environment, 2) comparing to operating norms, 3) initiating appropriate action, and repeating the cycle. Double-loop learning depends on being able to take a second look by questioning the relevance of the operating norms. The double-loop is created by adding another loop (to the second step) to discern whether the operating norms are appropriate.

The Need for Policy Review

FIGURE 1-1
SINGLE-LOOP AND DOUBLE-LOOP LEARNING

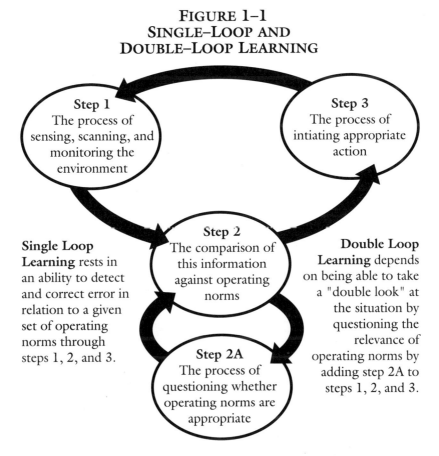

The double-loop learning idea provides some insight into the need for Plenary Review. For example, Congress is somewhat proficient in identifying policy problems, enacting individual programs or policies, and overseeing general performance. This is single-loop operation. In a double-loop learning (or Plenary Review) approach, Congress would identify policy problems, enact individual programs and policies—and then periodically create a second loop (or mode) in which they would question assumptions, assess macro-policy consequences and consider anew the appropriateness of goals as prescribed and practiced. Plenary Review is not intended to improve current policy details as much as it is intended to be a more general, reflective, retrospective assessment of the consequences of policy results. On the basis of such knowledge, prescription of public purposes and adjusting action can be devised. The importance of the concept of double-loop learning for the American public policy system is that it allows Congress and other players to evaluate general policy consequences and to take prospective action. Just as double-loop learning would benefit congressional performance, so would it be of benefit to all other bodies with public policy responsibilities.

Some modern organizational theorists see the most critical dimension of organization to be its capacity of "learning to learn" (Morgan, 1986: 87-99). This concept applies equally well to the functioning of our political framework's many policy subsystems. Unfortunately, the systems may function without adequately learning from experience and without turning such learning into system improvements. If Congress and other bodies in the policy system were to develop an improved capacity to learn, they would be better able to assess impacts, note results and take appropriate actions. Plenary Review is designed to respond to this need. It can be seen, in part, as ongoing learning about operation and impact. Such learning to learn would be characterized by value openness, reflectivity, acceptance of error and adjustment, exploration, inquiry-driven action and adaptation (Morgan, 1986: 87-99). Plenary Review will be presented as a decision process to help policy bodies evaluate their performance through assessing the general consequences of the policies enacted and to take appropriate action. It is learning by doing and then doing from learning.

Closely related to "learning to learn" is the concept of "social learning." Clarence Stone has argued that social learning is more than a simple effort to adapt policy initiatives to implementation needs in the political environment and is more than an improved institutional memory. Instead, in his view, social learning should be understood as increased understanding of social policy and problems (1986: 495). Others see social learning as critical in adapting our political and organizational systems to a pressing future (Korten, 1981). The concept of social learning simply reinforces the need in our public policy system for adaptive learning.

The Need for Organic Adaptation

The metaphor of the organism has been very powerful in the development of organizational theory (Morgan, 1986: 39-76). This metaphor helps also to understand the need for Plenary Review. The policy process may be viewed as a living system which interacts with the demands in its context. It may usefully be seen as a process rather than a collection of parts or institutions. Survival of the polity is dependent on the policy process recognizing and responding to needs (in organic adaptation rather than as rational goals to be pursued). There is a need to enable public policy decision systems to better understand needs and changing environmental demands. In a Plenary Review approach, public policy bodies would better receive feedback on the consequences of their public policy actions and would better adapt to their contexts.

The Need for Steering

Cybernetics is the study of information and communication as used to control and guide (the term is derived from the Greek for steersman). Self-regulation through information and communication occurs largely through negative feedback and error correction. Steering includes sensing and monitoring, relating this to the norms that guide system behavior, detecting deviation and taking corrective action (Morgan, 1986: 86-87). Effective steering of the polity is not well performed in our current public policy system.

Russell Ackoff's concept of interactivism (1974: 22) adds action (proactivity) to the notion of steering. Ackoff sees different responses to challenges. Inactivism does nothing; reactivism lets events determine basic approaches. "Preactivism" is an attempt to predict and prepare, but it also plans for the future rather than planning the future. As an orientation, interactivism seeks to respond to the challenges, not just react to or accept them. It seeks fundamental changes and attempts to control the system and steer its direction rather than accept an imposed direction and cope with its results. This interactive approach is not characteristic of most policy decisions; there is a need to meet future demands proactively. It is critical that we better perceive policy needs in a way that changes the premises and guides the future.

In brief, it is critical that we develop a capacity to learn from past policy practices, to take a second look at operating assumptions, to learn how to learn and respond at the level of governance, to adapt to the challenges of our context much as an organism must, to develop better self-direction, to steer our polity in directions desired, and to interactively respond to the challenges we face. These capacities are critical to effective governance and survival. Plenary Review will be presented as a policy mode to help meet these challenges.

Summary

The premise of this Chapter is that there are some great challenges and needs confronting the public policy system. The decision processes currently used to determine public policy are not adequate to deal with these concerns. One must think boldly of new policy modes to meet the magnitude of the challenge. The contentions of this chapter can be summarized in the following points.

The Chapter presented four central needs which animate the effort to make improvements in the approach to public policy. The first need arises because the social, moral, economic, political and institutional consequences of public policies are not adequately assessed on a periodic basis in most legislative and organizational contexts. The second stems from the concern that public policies are not adequately reviewed to identify interrelationships and establish coherent integrated policy. The third need exists because general public purposes and guiding macro-policies are not established. The fourth need contends that policy leadership actions are inadequate to enable effective adjustment and adaptation.

Metaphors also provide insight into critical needs in the public policy decision process. The metaphors of adaptive learning and double-loop learning suggest the need for decision makers to perceive the general direction of policies, assess consequences, deliberate desirable alternatives and establish guiding actions. The metaphor of the organism illustrates the need for better recognizing and adapting to challenges and changes in the context. Employing the cybernetic metaphor of steering, the policy system needs to gather information effectively, relate to guiding norms and pilot the system.

Many of the public policies enacted and applied in our current system are not adequate to the policy challenges which face the polity. There is not adequate action and leadership in many areas of public policy. There is a limited understanding of the changing context. Inadequacies in public policy are undermining the authority and legitimacy of the governance system. These concerns lead to the proposal of Plenary Review in the following chapter as a bold idea for Congress and other public institutions to deal with these needs and to rise to public policy challenges.

Two:
The Core Elements of Plenary Review

There is a great need for public policy deliberations at a higher level of generality, which some call macro-policy or governance level policy. Plenary Review is proposed as a separate policy mode which considers the general principles of government which guide statutory law, programs, policies and the administration of laws. This level considers the ends to which policy is the means and it deliberates underlying justifications and public purposes. As a *macro-policy* mode, Plenary Review assesses the general consequences of past policy action, deliberates broad public purposes and directs prospective actions to achieve desired ends. Debates in the legislative, organizational, public and academic arenas normally focus on the particulars of the public policies at issue. These *micro-policy* concerns (which deal with individual programs and statutes) are necessary and important, but there are also critical, though frequently unrecognized, macro-policy concerns which should receive regular attention by the responsible policy body. Plenary Review is not intended to replace micro-policy efforts, but rather to be a complementary and guiding mode to the current policy mode.

Although it will vary some according to the context in which it is applied, Plenary Review can contribute a great deal to bodies engaged in making policy and overseeing organizational performance. These include legislative public policy bodies (such as Congress, state legislatures, city councils and public boards) and executive public policy bodies (including presidential, gubernatorial, departmental and administrative agencies). Plenary Review may also be used in bodies which discuss public policy (such as citizen forums and classrooms) and in private and non-profit organizations with the need to assess consequences of past policies and performance and to direct future action. A prime application for the Plenary Review concept is the Congress of the United States where the results of many public policies need to be assessed and challenges need to be met. Many of the illustrations used will focus on the U.S. Congress.

Although some applications of Plenary Review will be made to private and non-profit organizations, the focus of this book will be public policy and public sector organizations. Since Plenary Review is directed at the improvement of *public policy*, this important term should be clarified at the outset. This clarification is intended to broaden the definition of "public policy" to recognize that public policy is determined in many places and by many participants beyond formal statutory enactment. Public policy, as used here, includes the formal legislative enactment, its executive direction, its judicial interpretation and its administrative implementation. Public policies are the result of the accumulation of statutes, rules, regulations, interpretations and practices over many years. They are often the *de facto* result of separate uncoordinated actions. Public policy is defined as that implemented as well as enacted, the informal as well as the formal. It is important to understand that public policy is more than a single statutory statement. Rather, public policy is the product of rich political processes, interorganizational actions and interpretations in many locations and at many stages.

The term *Plenary Review* is chosen to connote the various senses of the words and their roots. *Plenary* conveys such meanings as: full and complete (as in plenary session), capable of action and direction, and empowered and responsible (as in plenipotentiary). *Review* is chosen to connote such meanings as: survey, inspection, encompassing and critical evaluation (as for a book or play), and retrospective view.

Plenary Review is best described by its essential characteristics. This might be considered an operational definition (see Honadle, 1986). The characteristics or elements presented here provide a gen-

The Core Elements of Plenary Review

eralized description of central considerations, similar to what is sometimes described as an ideal type or pure model (which terminology is purposely not used to escape some of the implications often associated with ideal and pure). These characteristics describe Plenary Review, but they should not be understood as constituting a technique or definition which is simply "plugged in" to a particular situation. As with any ideal type, any one particular application of Plenary Review may or may not reflect each of these characteristics in its fully developed form. Plenary Review is intended to be an open, flexible, fully interactive process and not a rigid technique or constraining format. These characteristics should be seen as elements which add particular and important influences, now insufficiently present in the policy-making process, to achieve an end result which is beneficial. Plenary Review will generally reflect the characteristics described here.

TABLE 2-1
PLENARY REVIEW CHARACTERISTICS

Assessment of Consequences
- Social, economic, moral, political and institutional consequences

Periodic Review
- Regularly revisiting the policy arena

Broad Perspective
- At a higher level of generality

Coherent and Integrated
- Coordinating related policies and programs

Guiding Direction
- Macro-policy to guide future actions

An explicit, limited, narrow definition of Plenary Review will purposely not be developed. Rather, this chapter will serve to describe, not define. Many concepts do not lend themselves to exact definitions. Even the apparently simple term "organization" has been the target of hundreds of definitional attempts, and there continue to be significant disagreements among different disciplines and literatures about precisely what constitutes an organization. Too detailed a definition might well so constrict the concept as to suffocate it. For the moment, the focus will be the essential characteristics of Plenary Review; issues of feasibility and operation will be held in abeyance for following chapters.

The following sections will present Plenary Review as a public policy mode characterized by 1) the assessment of economic, social, moral, political and institutional consequences, 2) periodic review, 3) evaluation at the macro-policy level for the broad perspective, 4) coherent and integrated policy, and 5) establishment of guiding public purposes for subsequent adaptive action. These five characteristics are listed in Table 2-1 and are discussed and their contribution to the policy process outlined in the following sections.

ASSESSMENT OF CONSEQUENCES

A critical element of Plenary Review is the *assessment* of the past and prospective *consequences* of public policy. The assessment of consequences structures consideration and informs deliberation by asking the most important questions: what have been the impact and outcome of specific policies and what are now the desirable consequences which can be sought in future policy decisions? The Plenary Review policy mode seeks first to evaluate current public policy in terms of its economic, social, moral, political and institutional consequences, as a prelude to subsequent policy redirection, amendment or change. This emphasis gives Plenary Review a strong results orientation. Such an examination evaluates the present consequences of past enactments and then attempts to forecast and guide the consequences to be achieved. The character of such an undertaking is definitely not technical policy analysis but a more general and normative form of inquiry.

Plenary Review can be seen in part as a policy mode which focuses on ethical, moral and other important questions. In fact, Plenary Review is a decision-framing or question-framing approach as well as a decision-making approach. It is a mode which considers the "ought." Since beliefs, ultimate goals, ends and such are important to consider, Plenary Review does not rely on much of the current methodology in the policy sciences. Plenary Review is necessarily not a rational, decision-making approach, but rather a deliberative, non-linear, judgmental, philosophical endeavor focused on a higher level of public policy generality. Public bodies must consider moral choices based on an assessment of consequences. Etzioni maintained that such a broad view is important as he argued, for example, that economic matters must be understood at a larger level that is encompassing of society, polity, culture and other factors (Etzioni, 1988: 3). In *Ethics for Policymaking: A Methodological Analysis*, Meehan noted the need for these broader considerations in policy making when he wrote that "The challenge facing those who favor traditional "democratic" principles is to create a governmental system that is able to achieve the level of performance that such assumptions require" (Meehan, 1990: 216).

One advantage of Plenary Review's focus on consequences is that is serves to expand rapidly the range, depth, dimensions and considerations which will fall within each individual's calculus of personal interest and decision. Systematic careful consideration of both the general principles on which present public policy is predicated and the difficulties and results of efforts to implement it will inform deliberation and judgements. This focus should help direct policy makers away from limited parochial considerations. For example, policy discussions of deficit reduction, deregulation, welfare, farm support and many other policy areas will be enriched by the focus on social, moral, political, economic and institutional consequences. The review of specific programs such as enterprise zones and Urban Development Action Grants (UDAG) will benefit from a review of the consequences of urban development generally.

The assessment of past and prospective consequences in Plenary Review will focus a policy body in an important but subtle manner. Eidelberg asked "what enables the genuine statesman to see what the ordinary man does not see?" (1974: 19). How can a statesman discern a questionable act in a legislative consideration while an ordinary man does not see the danger? Eidelberg answered that "a good man, precisely because he is good, is concerned about the consequences of his actions, and for others as well as for himself . . . he will weigh alternative courses of action . . . [and] consider immediate and long-range consequences." Such assessment of consequences is intended to assist in informing judgement and in providing a guiding vision for the future. In times of adversity, Dror has maintained, policy making needs to be "result-directed" rather than "conduct-oriented" (1986: 55). And MacRae, in his book on policy indicators, argued that "outcome values are the test of information systems" (1985: 9-13).

Although it may appear solely abstract, the focus on consequences provides the pragmatic and practical orientation of Plenary Review.

Stephen Toulmin, in a thoughtful article on "The Recovery of Practical Philosophy," has argued that examining the practical context and the consequences of any particular question makes all the difference (Toulmin, 1988). For example, it does not matter what you answer to an abstract or philosophical question such as "Is a flying boat a ship or an airplane?" But the issues come better into focus when the context is practical and the consequences are clear: "Ought the captain of a flying boat have an airline pilot's license, a master mariner's certificate, or both?" Problems which are unsolvable in the abstract can be handled more adequately in the practical and specific. The focus on past and prospective consequences makes issues practical and timely rather than questions of eternal verities, and makes them concrete and case specific rather than merely abstract, particular rather than universal. Consequences are not assessed in a vacuum, but within the experience of past policy and its projection into the future.

The assessment of consequences is important because it must lead to discussions and judgements beyond only the rational and the economic. Although many shy from selecting guiding values for public issues and from assessing the social, moral, political, economic and institutional consequences, these are at the core of Plenary Review and of effective policy-making. Robert Sagoff, of the Center for Philosophy and Public Policy at the University of Maryland, has illustrated the importance of incorporating normative values into public policy. In *The Economy of the Earth*, for example, he has argued persuasively that environmental policies must be treated in a conceptual and normative way. Sagoff contended that "the role of the policy-maker, indeed, of the legislature—and derivatively the role of the courts—may be to balance what we believe in and stand for as a community with what we want and need to achieve as a functioning economy.... It is not just a matter of balancing interests with interests; it is a matter of balancing interests with morality and balancing one morality with another morality" (1988: 98).

The significant public policy questions are usually those which are prescriptive and normative. While policy analysts can add to the discourse, they face the limits of current techniques and the rigidity of their methodologies. Sagoff argued that "the quest for certainty—the vision of science as revealing Truth rather than as solving problems—tempts analysts to try to develop theories, models and mathematical criteria as ways to resolve practical and political problems on a rational basis" (1988: 12-13). Policy analysts enmeshed in this methodology and this vision of science, Sagoff observed, can well build academic careers but offer too little to public policy. Program evaluation techniques cannot make the necessary value judgements for program decisions (Abt, 1976: 13). There is a real and continuing need for effective assessment of consequences in normative terms and for normative prescriptions in developing public policy.

Value concerns can indeed guide choices among specific objectives and programs. Duncan MacRae has proposed that end-values enter into public debate as guides to reconciliation of tradeoffs among more specific values, that they be used as possible policy indicators, and that they be used to link the political and expert communities in a common discourse (1985: 15). MacRae illustrated the difference between focusing on end-values and contributory variables (1985: 38-39). By way of example in the area of health and illness, end-values would focus on health as perfection, length of life and quality-adjusted life years. Debate and evaluation focused on contributory variables would note incidence of diseases and services rendered. In Plenary Review, the focus on values is important in orienting deliberative debate to the most significant questions and judgements. In a study of Congress, Arthur Maass urged this broader orientation (1983: 4 ff.). He rejected pluralist political approaches (partisan mutual adjustment, utility maximization and interest group pluralism) primarily because they considered the wrong specific questions. He used a research model which focused more generally on deliberation and discussion, the public good and the broader community interest. These, after all, are the most important questions.

The assessment of consequences will not mean that easy answers will be either available or readily forthcoming. The limits of mind and information will surely constrain the process, but at least Congress (or other policy body conducting a review) would be considering the significant general questions about the impacts of public policy. The availability of perfect analysis or alternatives need not be assumed. Plenary Review simply attempts just the best that diverse persons and imperfect processes can produce. Nor will the result be intended to stand for all time. Instead, Plenary Review is designed to be an ongoing assessment of consequences and guiding values, to be employed periodically to consider changing circumstances as they develop. Of course, analysis of outcomes is very often difficult and problematic (Levin & Ferman, 1985: 27-30). Positive indicators of outcomes can be rather scarce. The intentions of policy makers can be quite different from the outcomes which they produce; it can never be assumed that what happens was intended to happen. Precise causal linkages between policies and outcomes are always difficult to establish. Even so, these difficulties do not eliminate the need to focus on the consequences of determinative public policy. Even partial or attempted analyses can provide some useful information for the guidance of future policy making efforts. These are indeed much better than no analysis at all. An essential element of Plenary Review is the assessment of moral, social, economic, political and institutional consequences of past and prospective public policy.

PERIODIC REVIEW OF PUBLIC POLICY

Plenary Review is characterized by the *periodic review* of public policy. The assessment of the consequences of existing policies and the determination of prospective actions based on that review must be done on a regular and repeating basis. Ideally, Plenary Review would establish a cycle for periodic review of all major policy areas. Until that point, there will still be benefit from Plenary Review performed on selected policy arenas. The interval is not as important as the mode, but it might be appropriate for Congress and other policy bodies to perform such an overview every seven to ten years. The important point is that the sovereign body reviews the consequences of policy actions at this higher level of generality in general policy areas on a regular basis and takes appropriate action.

It is important that the review of public policy include matters beyond the statutory statement. As it considers the statutes and public law, in a topical area, it should also review related rules, regulations, interpretations and implementing decisions. It should consider both formal and informal decisions which issue from executive, legislative, judicial and administrative actors. Plenary Review must cover administrative directives and actual practice since public policy necessarily is modified, interpreted, ignored, updated, hindered or improved as part of its implementation. With Plenary Review, both the intended and unintended results of policy implementation come under review. Where there have been previous Plenary Reviews, these will also be taken into account.

Ideally, the policy body should schedule the periodic review of public policies in a separate mode of operation. That is, the policy body could regularly move from a legislative (or regular policy) mode to a Plenary Review mode in order to conduct the periodic review. A scheduled Plenary Review mode would provide the time and focus for periodic review. For example, Congress would step into a Plenary Review mode to review the consequences of various policies, programs, rules and regulations in general policy areas such as the environment, banking and financial regulation, tax policy, education, employment and training programs and so forth.

The periodic nature of the review is intended as a force for action and change. When fully successful, Plenary Review would provide a periodic assessment of what has been done in general policy terms, what the consequences have been and what adjustments are necessary to meet the future effectively. This level of consideration is required because current challenges in the polity go well beyond the capacity of an incremental, accidental or *ad hoc* policy process to address them. Yehezkel Dror has argued that "present policy predicaments . . . do require considerable systems transformation" (1986: 94). If present features of our policy-making and reviewing systems are seen to be static or susceptible only to incremental change, Dror concluded, there may be little hope for the improvements needed to meet policy problems (Dror, 1986: 231). Plenary Review is proposed as a means to institute broadscale periodic review of public policy followed by a deliberate response based on that review.

Because legislatures are the primary policy analysis mechanisms in government (Dreyfus, 1976: 269), Plenary Review is particularly directed toward legislative use. The objective of Plenary Review is to increase the capacity of legislative bodies to sense regularly general trends and needs, assess consequences, articulate options and determine the collective will as the responsible decision maker. It is axiomatic that the power to enact laws inherently carries with it the responsibility to review their consequences and to enact appropriate adjustments. In systems terminology, output performance should result in feedback to allow adaptation. Democratic ideology requires such governing control and direction by the elected representatives of the people (Scher, 1963: 526).

Even if all policy arenas are not completed in a comprehensive schedule, much benefit may still be obtained from any reviews performed and from a review cycle only partially followed. For example, the congressional budget procedures in recent years have attempted to impose assigned tasks and dates. These have not been followed faithfully, but the process nevertheless has benefitted from the attempt.

The result of the Plenary Review process will not be an overpowering analysis which convinces all persons of exactly what ought to be done. It will, however, better develop those important issues which can lead to a determination of where the system currently is and where it should go as best can be ascertained at that time. In the phrase used earlier, Plenary Review is a periodic and systematic attempt to "learn to learn." Congressional Plenary Review is intended as a format to help Congress periodically focus attention on each important policy area in order to evaluate outcomes as best possible and to take appropriate actions. The hopeful Socratic assumption— that knowledge can be obtained and thus answers found—may sometimes disappoint, but the consequences are no worse than avoiding a responsible examination of past and prospective consequences and not providing guidance to the future.

MACRO–POLICY AND A BROADER PERSPECTIVE

In addition to periodic review and assessment of consequences, the scope and level of analysis undertaken in Plenary Review are important. Plenary Review is not fine-tuning, nor detailed program oversight, but a *broad perspective* or *macro-policy*—standing back for a more objective and encompassing view at a higher level of generality. It is an evaluative overview designed to provide an encompassing long-range view, to look beyond incremental actions and to improve the general outcomes of prospective policy actions. The level of evaluation is architectural design, not plumbing or electrical wiring.

The broader view includes two aspects. First, the level of generality distinguishes Plenary Review from other responses in the policy system. The Plenary Review focus is general policy arenas—rather than just particular programs, specific policies or short-term responses. It looks at groups of programs, arenas of related policies and intersections among policies. For example, Plenary Review would consider urban development policy and its various intersecting and overlapping policies and programs, rather than the Urban Development Action Grant (UDAG) program. Plenary Review adds another mode at a higher level to complement routine policy analysis, legislative enactments and executive review. A policy body, such as the U.S. Congress, would periodically change from the regular mode of policy decisions to take the broader macro-view in a Plenary Review mode. Second, the macro-policy approach, as discussed in previous sections, deliberates general purposes and principles which guide subsequent debate, enactment and implementation of specific policies and programs.

The Core Elements of Plenary Review

One interesting way to think about the broad perspective used in Plenary Review is to speculate what comments Alexis de Tocqueville might make were he observing 1990 instead of 1830 and what Max Weber might have written had his studies begun in 1990 rather than 1890. Weber, who understood well the liabilities as well as the benefits of bureaucracy, might be concerned with narrow bureaucratic decision making and limited policy vision (Morrill, 1989; Jackall, 1988). He would probably see outcomes from our various policies, programs and institutions which we miss. De Tocqueville might have commented on the challenges facing governance and the limited ability of current decision processes and institutions to establish coherent public policy. He may have seen societal and moral impacts which are more dim to us. The broader perspective characteristic of de Tocqueville and Weber illustrate the level of analysis in Plenary Review.

The broader perspective is designed to provide an encompassing long-range view and to look beyond incremental actions. For example, the savings and loan crisis may be seen as the direct consequence of public policy without regular review and the unrecognized outcome of past policies such as policies on home ownership and deposit insurance.

The broad scope and long-term view are important to the effectiveness of public policy. This is the need James MacGregor Burns recognized when he agreed with the Panel on the Electoral and Democratic Process (of the President's Commission for a National Agenda for the Eighties) that "there has to be a way of melding the members [of Congress] into a policy-making body; there has to be a way to encourage them to compromise some short-term interests for the long-term interests of the nation" (Burns, 1984: 173). Arthur Maass has also contended that the public interest is related to breadth of view (1983: 18). And Arthur Macmahon noted the need for such an encompassing view when he said that "the hazard is that a body like Congress, when it gets into detail, ceases to be itself" (Matthew & Stimson, 1975: 159).

This need for the broad view underlies other congressional initiatives which have struggled toward a similar end. The reform of the congressional budget process may be seen as one such attempt (Ellwood, 1985: 315). Another attempt—although generally ignored by Congress—was a provision for a broad periodic review of grant programs in the 1968 Intergovernmental Cooperation Act. And, Ripley reports that a number of studies have moved toward the overview rather than the details of congressional oversight (1987: 222-223). Walter Oleszek has noted a surge of interest in general review and evaluation in the 1980's stemming from heightened public concern and dissatisfaction, distrust resulting from policy events (Vietnam, Watergate, etc.), election of legislators skeptical about public programs, the proliferation of federal programs and regulations, fiscal scarcity, expert and special interest group efforts and expansion of congressional staff (1984: 235-236).

At first contact, some may confuse Plenary Review with legislation, oversight or sunset review. While some similarity among the functions exists, Plenary Review is distinctive in level, objective, scope and timing from legislation, oversight and sunset review. Oversight, strictly defined, is the process of determining whether executive agencies carry out programs as Congress intended (US Subcommittee on Oversight, 1976: 10-11). Its focus is on particulars of existing policy rather than general policies (Huntington, 1965: 25). Oversight is more a check on performance—how something is implemented—rather than a general review of public law and its consequences. Beyond the level of oversight is the need to deal with questions of consequences, impacts, philosophy and coherence. This is the level of focus attempted in Plenary Review.

The distinction between congressional oversight and Plenary Review can be further drawn from the models suggested by McCubbins and Schwartz (1984: 165-179). They sketched two general models of oversight: fire alarm and police patrol. Congress—for reasons of rationality and time—prefers the fire alarm model of oversight. Almost all oversight in Congress has been in the fire alarm mode of reacting to emergencies and arising needs. This response is uncoordinated, decentralized and selective. The police patrol oversight model is more coordinated, active, comprehensive and direct. In this one aspect, Plenary Review may be seen as an attempt to add another model of policy review—the police patrol.

The sunset review approach requires that particular pieces of legislation be reviewed after a specific period (usually seven years). Since the act expires if not renewed, the policy body is forced to undertake a review and make a decision. Sunset review is similar to Plenary Review in the periodic aspect, but different in that it does not integrate related areas or take a macro-policy view.

TABLE 2-2
COMPARISON OF CONGRESSIONAL MODES

Item	Legislative Mode	Oversight Mode	Sunset Review Mode	Plenary Review Mode
Objective	To enact statutes on specific programs and appropriations	To review executive and agency operations which implement legislation	To review periodically specific programs and agencies to extend or discontinue	To assess periodically consequences, establish macro-policy for future direction
Level	Specific policies and programs	Specific policies and programs	Specific policies and programs	Policy arenas, macro-policy
Scope	Immediate period	Immediate period	Long-range	Long-range
Focus	Specific policies and programs	Agency performance	Policy and agency performance	Social, moral, economic, political consequences
Timing	Continual, piecemeal	Intermittent, not scheduled	Scheduled periodic review	Scheduled periodic review

To distinguish better among these congressional functions, Table 2-2 contrasts Plenary Review with the regular congressional mode of legislation, the sunset review mode and the oversight mode.

As illustrated in Table 2–2, Plenary Review is a separate mode of review by a legislature or other policy body. There is benefit, of course, in a Plenary Review perspective enriching all policy decisions, but the full application of Plenary Review requires a separate decision mode in the policy body. For example, Congress should periodically step out of the legislative mode into a Plenary Review mode. This mode permits a more reflective assessment of consequences and deliberation of public purposes and the objective, level, scope, focus and timing necessary for Plenary Review. Congress usually works in an incremental and piecemeal fashion. The Plenary Review mode considers the broader view, the larger picture.

MORE COHERENT AND INTEGRATED POLICY ARENAS

The periodic broad review of consequences in the Plenary Review mode enables the development of the next element: *more coherent and more integrated* public policy. Policy enactments accumulated over years do not necessarily combine into a coherent and integrated whole and related policies and practices are often not compared and reconciled. The scope of review is the *arena* of related policies. The integration of related policies and programs is designed to establish essential policy coherence and consistency and to determine better desired public policy outcomes for the future.

As the reader has noticed, the Plenary Review characteristics overlap and interrelate. This element can be distinguished from the one discussed in the previous section by thinking of one as vertical and the other as horizontal. The broader perspective is a vertical construct to assess at a higher level of generality. More integrated and coherent policy is a horizontal construct to relate to other policies and actions. Macro-policy encompasses both the higher guiding policy and the interrelation of specific programs and policies.

This horizontal integration is important to compare related policies and programs and to identify areas of complementation and conflict. Competing policies which seek opposite ends are particularly important to identify and consider. For example, one policy may encourage home ownership while another hinders it; one program may encourage tobacco consumption while another attempts to de-

The Core Elements of Plenary Review

crease it. The consistency and coherence of related policies is also important in establishing the broader perspective and developing an evaluative policy framework.

This Plenary Review element attempts to avoid some of the policy consequences of fragmentation. Our current fragmented policy system is characterized by slow change, low concern with bureaucratic performance, and a generally passive stance toward action (see Ripley, 1983: 12-18). An integrated and coherent policy approach, on the other hand, tries to design an enhanced ability to change, to consider major redirections, and to evaluate policy impact.

Congress may again be used to illustrate this point. James Sundquist has observed the need for policy integration in Congress (1981: 429-439). He reported some integrative attempts based on centralized control, but these have not been long lasting or effective. The "centrifugal forces of individualism have gained strength with every passing year," Sundquist commented, and policy integration *between* the two houses of Congress "is a territory almost wholly unexplored" (1981: 438). There have been very few attempts at bicameral policy integration; he cited the Committee of Fifteen on Reconstruction, the Joint Committee on Atomic Energy (now abolished) and the Joint Economic Committee (which has not had legislative jurisdiction). The new budget process has had some impact on fiscal policy, and Sundquist noted, it could work in theory in other policy areas such as urban growth policy and energy policy. One of the most promising innovations for congressional policy integration and planning, Sundquist reported, has been the use (in the House of Representatives) of ad hoc committees with legislative jurisdiction (1981: 432-435).

Randall Ripley has noted that fragmentation maximizes the function of representation, while a higher degree of integration would maximize lawmaking and policy determination (1983: 22). He has argued that a high degree of fragmentation is most likely to be the case in our governmental system. This "natural" state of Congress requires little or no deliberate action to create or sustain. On the other hand, a high degree of integration is difficult, but not impossible to achieve. An "unnatural" state, it would require considerable deliberate action. Ripley concluded that "integration does not guarantee systematic attention to oversight or evaluation but does enhance the chances" that such can occur (1983: 15-16). Plenary Review has the objective of creating a mode where deliberate effort can be given to integrated and coherent policy.

The term *policy arena* is used to define an area of related policies. The level of review must be larger than single programs to capture the intersection and interdependence of different policies and to seek consistency in related policies. On the other hand, the arena of relationship must be circumscribed because a scope too broad may lack meaning and encompass too much for effective comparison. For example, the focus might be on the consequences of banking legislation and practices, rather than an individual banking statute. The policy body will have to determine the policy arenas to be used (some suggestions will be discussed in a later chapter). Not only should the various pieces of legislation and programs be compared and reconciled, the rules, regulations, interpretations, practices and operations in different public policy actions need to be related to one another.

Plenary Review would establish a process to enable integration and coherence in various policy arenas. Note, for example, how the new budget process in Congress established mechanisms, cycles and institutions to coordinate effort, assign responsibilities, and establish comprehensive evaluation and control. The format provided a broad view (including a look at the impact of the budget) and the establishment of guidelines. The general guidelines were then used to direct and coordinate all other actions and decisions, although they could be modified. In similar fashion, Plenary Review will enable more coherent and integrated policy through its focus and format. This policy then gives guidance to other more specific policy actions. Although it can be modified as circumstances warrant, reference to it will inform and improve specific policy and program decisions.

Guiding Direction and Adaptive Action

The outcome of the Plenary Review mode takes the form of a *guiding direction*. This statement of macro-policy is the Plenary Review action of the policy body, such as Congress or a state legislature. A guiding direction includes the deliberative body's finding concerning public policy consequences, provides a statement of guiding purposes and outlines actions to remedy perceived difficulties and to establish appropriate changes. Statutory enactments and other policy statements normally focus on the particular; their statement is detailed. Plenary Review enactments are broad public policy generalizations for future application; their statement provides an overarching guideline or macro-policy. In Plenary Review, the guiding philosophy, determination of desired outcomes and evaluation of consequences establish the context for subsequent programmatic legislation, rules, regulations and administrative interpretations. Thus, the "sense of the representative assembly" in its Plenary Review guiding directive would provide some coherence and macro-policy direction within which other actions would take place. Unlike the Constitution, however, the Plenary Review direction would be open to revision and adjustment at the time of each specific legislative or policy enactment. Its prime requirement would be that reference be made to the guiding macro-policy direction in any legislative and policy actions within the policy arena being considered.

The guiding direction—to use Dror's term—establishes the "central mind of government" and the "central policy will" (1986: 4). Plenary Review deals with these more central—indeed almost philosophical—concerns. In the deliberation within policy arenas, Congress will necessarily have to grapple with overarching concerns— such as system stability, appropriate prospective boundaries between governmental regulation and the free market, and moral and social consequences of specific policies and programs.

For example, a guiding direction on employment policy might assess the social, moral, political, economic and institutional consequences of the various programs, policies, regulations and agency actions which relate to employment. The direction would state the general purposes which employment, training and other programs within the policy arena should achieve. Ends criteria might be specified to guide future policies and actions. As appropriate, corrective actions can be directed to which the various programs and policies would conform. A partial example was the Full Employment Act of 1946, which specified the policy of full employment and established the mechanism of the federal budget to create full employment through its impact on the economy.

Plenary Review is a forward look concerning what ought to occur in a policy arena and providing guidance for actions toward that end.   In an important sense, Plenary Review may be considered a form of strategic thinking, aimed at developing a constructive response to changing conditions well based on an evaluation of the context and the outcomes of past and current actions. This need not require a large and involved process, extensive information or far-ranging staff support. Many corporations have found that strategic thinking does not require major planning and analytical units; some of the most outstanding corporate performances have issued from relatively small strategic planning staffs (Toft, 1986: 250).

Plenary Review is an attempt to provide guiding directions to improve and inform subsequent specific policy enactments. It is an attempt to provide conscious direction to the governance system and to confront the most important philosophical and political questions.

The Plenary Review Decision Process

The core elements of Plenary Review have been discussed in the preceding sections on assessment of consequences, periodic review macro-policy, integrated perspective and guiding direction. In addition to these core elements, there are some process characteristics of Plenary Review to be discussed. These characteristics are important in enabling the decision process to achieve Plenary Review goals: 1) participation and deliberation, 2) requirement for a decision, and 3) quantitative resolution of disagreements. The following sections focus on the basic concepts; operational concerns will be developed in a later chapter.

The Deliberative Process

The separate Plenary Review mode works best through a *participative and deliberative process*. The struggle of opinion and information in a deliberative format can best consider important questions and establish general guiding principles or macro-policy. The dynamics of participative discussion in the Plenary Review mode help to convert the decision process from the necessary and proper limitations of partisan, parochial and often unexamined interests in considering specific legislation into a more encompassing examination of the collective future interest. It encourages participants to look beyond their initial positions through considering the moral, social, economic, political and institutional consequences of policy. Plenary Review expands the range, depth and dimensions of the policy map of participants through wide consideration of both the general principles on which a policy has been (and should be) predicated and implemented. The deliberative format results in the development of more creative alternatives for future policy action. Since Plenary Review is not fine-tuning, but rather a broad evaluation of policy, broad discussion is important to the approach and outcome.

Method and approach influence thought. Methodology defines the science. The matters considered and not considered and the way information and views are presented and compared are influenced by the process. In the physical sciences, the methodology is the guiding framework for the results of investigation. In the political and social sciences, the influence of the process employed is essentially corrective, both allowing for and encouraging the interaction of the plurality of forces at work. This is illustrated by the technique of brainstorming: analyzing, thinking, building and creating are most productive in open and flowing discussion; evaluation and decision should follow rather than limit the unfolding considerations. The effect of the deliberative process has been nicely described by Paul Eidelberg:

> When a legislator engages in debate, the arguments he advances are necessarily biased in favor of his own interests (which bear some relationship, of course, to those of his constituents). In principle, there is nothing reprehensible about this. The common good itself requires the emphatic articulation of particular interests which, to be sure, must be mutually adjusted in the process of deliberation. . . . Deliberation—and I shall be speaking of deliberation at its best—reveals the mutual obstructiveness yet interdependence of emphatically articulated interests. . . . By emphasizing his own interest, each legislator may contribute to the good of another, provided only that a common course of action can be agreed upon. . . . Objectivity thus turns on a mind whose subjectivity embraces a whole more comprehensive in its values than that perceived by others. (Eidelberg, 1974.)

As this discussion is applied to the national government, it may seem a bit strange to call for a deliberative process in the United States Congress. After all, the Senate has often been referred to as the "greatest deliberative body" in the world. However, it is increasingly difficult to describe the Congress as a deliberative decisionmaker. There are infrequent "great debates;" the usual routine is set speeches made to an empty floor. There often is rather little give and take. While there are reasons for (and some strengths in) the fragmentation and specialization of Congress, an important political cost has been a decrease in capacity for and concern with broad policy and general administrative performance (Maass, 1983: 41-42). Senator Nancy Kassebaum reported that the Senate no longer is a great deliberative body and that great debate is only a memory (1985: A19). Norman Ornstein has observed that few members of Congress are satisfied with its work or its outputs (1985: 32). He noted that the Senate is neither a great deliberative body nor an efficient processor of laws; he concluded that the nation's upper house is an institution in search of an identity. Steven Smith reported that in "neither chamber of Congress does floor discussion achieve the ideal of either debate or deliberation" (1989: 239).

The increasing fragmentation of responsibility, decision and action has increasingly undermined the deliberative function. Price noted that with its committees and subcommittees, Congress has left its undisciplined parts in control of the pieces of business (1985: 132). Research reported by Parker indicated that there are more immediate benefits from work for constituents than from effective policy consideration (1985: 10). Another congressional scholar, Leroy Rieselbach, contended that structural decentralization and diffusion of authority result in less responsibility, less responsiveness and less accountability (1977: 32-33). The political and deliberative functions of Congress need to be protected; the concerns of organization and operation often deflect Congress from its essential purpose. Smith and Deering have noted that the primary effect of recent congressional changes has been the increased fragmentation of decision-making (1984: 1). And, Huntington has observed that power in the legislature has become increasingly fragmented and dispersed at a time of nationalizing changes in the system of governance (1965: 4-5). The irony is that committee government and fragmentation attempt to satisfy individual desires for power, but that they disperse authority so widely as to result in "institutional impotence" which "cripples the ability of Congress to perform its constitutional roles" (Dodd, 1985: 499).

Plenary Review does not presume to change the factors influencing policy discussions and decisions. For example, congressional voting will still be influenced by committee structure and procedures, party, ideology, district interests, past votes, issue development, presidential influence and other such factors (see Asher & Weisberg, 1985: 427-428). Votes will still be influenced by legislative colleagues (Matthews & Stimson, 1975: 150-160). Plenary Review attempts to add another deliberative mode to increase congressional effectiveness and enhance policy determinations.

Requirement for Decision

The Plenary Review mode requires a *decision*. Plenary Review is designed to be more than an analysis of programs grouped into policy arenas; a decision concludes the deliberations. The best choices

The Core Elements of Plenary Review 61

must be based on evaluation of the past and prospective consequences of public policy. The requirement for a decision is important in providing a focus and force to Plenary Review deliberations. Its discussions will not center on the most significant longer term questions without the requirement for a decision and action. The requirement for a decision gives a practical and a governance focus to Plenary Review since the decision is the enactment of the guiding direction. The Plenary Review requirement for a decision should also encourage action and stimulate leadership.

It matters less what is decided than that a review and decision must be made and that that decision must be periodically reviewed and adjusted. It is not important if no change is made, but it is critically important that the public policy body assess the consequences in each general policy arena, determine general purposes and confirm guiding directions. Without such a forcing mechanism—and leaving the operational problems to a later chapter, policy bodies can too often avoid timely review and action.

The requirement for a decision simply assists Congress and other policy bodies to rise to their inherent responsibility to take legislative action as the responsible empowered agent. Congress, acting within the constitutional framework, has the assignment of enacting policy directives, be they shorter term or longer term, be they in narrow policy areas or wider arenas where policies and purposes overlap. Congress would more closely function—in the words of Woodrow Wilson—as the "predominant and controlling force, the centre and the source of all motive and of all regulatory power" (1885: 11). Traditional democratic theory clearly places the responsibility for overview, consequences and authoritative actions with the Congress. Since Congress has both the responsibility and the power, the question becomes how to use that decision power more effectively (see Jones, 1975: 276; Sundquist, 1981: 367-414). Plenary Review and the requirement for a decision are designed to help Congress and other policy bodies rise to their leadership responsibilities.

Quantitative Resolution

The decision process used in Plenary Review can be brought to closure through the *quantitative vote* of the policy body. The Plenary Review mode does not presume that deliberation will result in consensus and that all will agree on the policy purposes to be pursued. There will be divergent viewpoints and most decisions will have to be reached by vote of the policy body.

The use of quantitative resolution is important for three reasons. First, it allows the body to reach a decision. And, as the previous section illustrated, a decision is important to influence the process. Second, it utilizes the processes for decision which already exist in policy bodies. Plenary Review does not require a new voting (or other) process for closure and decision. Third, qualitative decisions are difficult to reach without a quantitative vote.

Plenary Review deliberations must end with decisions on values. Some—including many social scientists—shy from complex and difficult questions of values and beliefs. Since values often raise the most significant questions, a decision format which attempts to be objective or neutral or to avoid value questions will fail to consider fully the important macro-policy issues (see Meehan, 1990). Plenary Review contends that the social, moral, economic, political and institutional consequences of policies must be regularly reviewed and evaluated and that a decision be made on a guiding direction (which is a selection of values).

Paul Eidelberg has argued that the inability to judge moral truths has led to the degradation of statesmanship (1974: 390). He has characterized the present as an age of "intellectual laissez-faire," a time rife with skepticism, an age in which people "have lost confidence in the power of the intellect to comprehend metaphysical and moral truths." Statesmanship and the challenges of the time nonetheless require making such decisions. At a time when most scholars focus on interaction of contending interests and "partisan mutual adjustment," for example, Arthur Maass enjoined the more important questions in his study of Congress by focusing on the public good as his model (1983: 19-28). The public interest, he contended, demands the necessary breadth of view. Of course, Congress necessarily engages in interest group bargaining, but the representative institution must be able to make decisions on the larger purposes if it is to perform its democratic function well.

Mark Sagoff, of the Center for Philosophy and Public Policy at the University of Maryland, has written persuasively about the need to consider goals and values (1988). Since policy expresses what we believe, he argued that the consideration of values is central to whom and what we are as a nation (1988: 16-17). Sagoff contended that we can deal with value questions in the public policy arena since each individual is a judge of values, not merely a haver of wants. It is not just interest against interest. The individual judges not merely for

The Core Elements of Plenary Review

himself but also as a member of relevant communities or groups. Of course values and beliefs are subjective, but they have objective social and political content as well. People make value judgements—or policy recommendations—on what they think is *right* not just what they *prefer*; it is claimed that such positions are *true*, not merely *felt* (1988: 43-55). Thus, Sagoff maintained that policy decisions in general can be judged on the basis of reason and warrants, not limited to wants and preferences (1988: 55). He illustrated how judgements and preferences in individuals can often diverge from wants when they join to support policy positions beyond their limited self-interest.

The Plenary Review approach argues that people are thinking beings in pursuit of their own interests, yet fully capable of discussing the values involved—both for themselves and others. As argued by Sagoff, public policies can be justified or refuted based on the judgements of what is said for and against them, not just the force of interest against interest, resolved by intensity of individual or group preferences. Public policy decisions, especially of the sort contemplated under the Plenary Review notion, must involve values. Plenary Review accepts the notion that intelligent discussion and weighing of values are possible. Public policy bodies, such as representative assemblies, must make policy decisions on value consequences.

Even while difficult, value decisions must be made. Resolution by quantitative vote is the traditional mechanism through which policy bodies have been able to make such decisions. But what about the quality of a decision arrived at through majority vote? Plenary Review does not assume perfect, or even optimum, decisions. The decisions resulting from Plenary Review are not expected to be perfect as they emanate from these deliberations. Rather, the process is designed to be a continual cycle of assessing policy consequences, making adjustments, assessing consequences and making adjustments. (The issue of Plenary Review decision rationality will be discussed in Chapter Three.)

Summary:
The Plenary Review Mode

Plenary Review is presented as general characteristics and elements rather than as a narrow technique. Similar to an ideal type, it can have many different applications, none of which may have all elements in their full form. Plenary Review may be described by the following core elements.

TABLE 2–3
PLENARY REVIEW
CORE ELEMENTS

Core Element	Design Objective
Plenary Review assesses the social, moral, economic, political and institutional consequences of public policy.	The assessment of consequences is designed to provide a practical results orientation, inform prospective action and expand the range of evaluation.
Plenary Review is the periodic review of public policy.	Periodic review is designed to enable policy bodies to assess regularly consequences, sense general needs and take appropriate actions.
Plenary Review focuses on the broader perspective and macro-policy, rather than detailed program oversight or individual policies.	The broader perspective is designed to provide an encompassing long-range view, to look beyond incremental actions and to improve the general outcomes of governance actions.
Plenary Review develops more coherent and integrated policy. It uses the concept of "policy arena" to consider interrelationships.	The integration of related policies and programs in policy arenas is designed to establish policy comparison and consistency.
The product of Plenary Review is a guiding direction which assesses consequences, states guiding policy purposes and directs prospective actions.	The guiding directive is designed to guide future policy actions and establish general macro-policy.

In addition to the core elements which describe Plenary Review, there are some characteristics which are important to the Plenary Review decision process. These process characteristics are the following.

The Core Elements of Plenary Review

TABLE 2-4
PLENARY REVIEW
PROCESS ELEMENTS

Process Element	Design Objective
Plenary Review is best conducted through a deliberative process.	The deliberative process is designed to fit most policy bodies and to facilitate evaluation and judgement.
Plenary Review prescribes that a decision conclude deliberations.	The requirement for a decision is designed to provide a pragmatic focus and action leadership.
Plenary Review decisions are made by the quantitative vote of the policy body.	The quantitative resolution of issues is designed to enable decisions and fit current processes of most policy bodies.

Decision makers and the public alike share an abiding concern to achieve effective governance and public policy. Plenary Review contributes to these goals through the assessment of consequences, periodic review of public policy as implemented, development of broader perspectives, increased coherence among related policy arenas, and establishment of guiding macro-policy purposes. The concepts which guide Plenary Review are applicable to many organizations and contexts, but are particularly designed for bodies—such as legislatures—which are responsible for public policy. In particular, the adoption of a Plenary Review mode in the Congress and other policy bodies could be a major benefit to their public policy responsibilities.

THREE: PLENARY REVIEW CONTRIBUTIONS TO PUBLIC POLICY DECISIONS

The Plenary Review concept prompts some crucial questions. How do Plenary Review elements contribute to the making of decisions on public policies? How does Plenary Review influence the legislative and other policy bodies which use it? Does Plenary Review produce superior decisions? Are Plenary Review decisions more rational than decisions in the regular policy mode? These important matters related to decision making will be discussed in this chapter.

A DECISION PROCESS FOR PUBLIC BODIES

Plenary Review is designed for public bodies with both the sovereign power and the responsibility to chart and assess a policy course. The Plenary Review decision process is directed to bodies where there is a basic need to step out of the mire of operational details and assess consequences, deliberate purposes, establish guiding actions and interrelate policies and programs into a more coherent whole. This includes legislative bodies such as Congress, state legislatures, city councils, school boards and other similar entities. It also can be used in executive bodies with public policy responsibilities. These would include cabinets, advisory committees, commissions, departmental staff groups, task forces and other bodies. (These applications will be developed further in later chapters.)

Plenary Review is a complementary mode of review to enable Congress and other policy bodies to be more effective in their broadscale policy responsibilities. Each mode of operation—Plenary Review and the regular policy mode—will have their own rationales and benefits, but they may complement each other well. The policy body (such as the United States Congress) would periodically step outside the usual policy (or legislative) mode to perform Plenary Review. Plenary Review insights and directions then feed back into and guide the policy process. It will be useful for the policy body to periodically step back to generalize and take the broad perspective; this then benefits the policy process. Plenary Review will institute a macro-policy perspective missing in current deliberations.

THE PRACTICAL FOCUS OF PLENARY REVIEW

Considering the points in the previous chapter, the presumption is sometimes made that Plenary Review is solely abstract and philosophical. However, Plenary Review is an interesting combination of the particular and the general, the practical and the philosophical. In addition to the broad philosophical aspects, Plenary Review as a decision process is very much rooted in the practical and applied. It is grounded in pragmatic decision making because it assesses specific consequences at the beginning and requires a decision and action at the end. It is based in experience. It agrees with the editorial statement of the *Journal of Public Policy* that "to understand public policy it is necessary to relate ideas to concrete problems of government." In *Ethics for Policymaking*, Meehan has argued that knowledge must have an action focus and that purposes can not be achieved without actions (1990: 7).

Plenary Review deals with past experience. It frames the initial questions in a thoroughly practical way. It assesses and then ascertains guiding purposes based on this experience. These public purposes guide future policy and subsequent programmatic action. If policy is defined narrowly as the specific laws and executive acts of government (Scruton, 1982: 358), then Plenary Review deals with those matters which generate policy and which describe the ends to which specific policy is the means.

The guiding direction developed through assessment of past and prospective consequences must be taken into account in future actions. The guiding direction may be accepted or it may be changed, but it must be consulted. In many ways, Plenary Review establishes a continuing process of policy generalization from past experience. Specific experience leads to a higher level of generalization in the guiding direction. These generalizations inform and guide future action. The generalizations must be dealt with as a court deals with precedent or the Constitution. Plenary Review is an analysis of what has gone on before. It is a re-generalization of what has happened and then a re-adjustment for future guidance. This periodic re-generalization can assist policy bodies to adjust and change public policies without waiting for crisis to force such change.

This periodic process of re-assessing experience and re-generalizing policy guidance combines the practical with the abstract. It draws from particulars to ascertain the general, then re-adjusts the generalization to guide the particulars. The interactivity of policy consequences and macro-policy is designed to enrich and refine each.

THE TRANSFORMING INFLUENCE OF PLENARY REVIEW

In Chapter Two, Plenary Review was described by noting the core elements of assessment of consequences, periodic review, macro-level focus, more integrated policy perspective, and establishment of guiding directions. These core elements lead to crucial questions: How do the Plenary Review core elements contribute to the concerns and needs of public bodies and their policies? How do the core elements of Plenary Review achieve the desired outcome?

Plenary Review exerts a transforming influence on the policy-making process and on the policy institutions which utilize it. The influence is not a result of simply inserting a tightly defined technique into the policy process. Rather, in recognition of the complexity of the process through which public policy is formed and implemented, the Plenary Review core elements are designed to stimulate broad perspectives, enable beneficial insights, encourage actions and inform outcomes. They are elements which will flavor and influence the policy process toward meeting the needs and challenges which have been identified in the first chapter. Plenary Review is a structuring influence to encourage and enable policy bodies to focus on critical questions and frame needed answers.

The decision approach affects the outcome so it is important to analyze the impact of the decision process itself. The methods and focus used for decision making have important consequences (Gortner, 1987: 244). The decision approach partially determines who participates, how agendas are established, which alternatives are considered, how they are compared and analyzed, and which values will dominate in the final selection. The procedures of decision making affect the substance of choice. For example, Popper has argued that the definition of a term such as democracy determines how the questions will be framed and how the responses will be determined (Popper, 1988: 21). Given the importance of the decision approach, this section will review the influence of Plenary Review on public policy decisions.

TABLE 3–1
INFLUENCE OF THE
ASSESSMENT OF CONSEQUENCES

The Assessment of Consequences Contributes to Plenary Review Because It:

- Expands considerations to include social, moral, political, economic and institutional consequences
- Provides feedback on both specific programs and general policies
- Identifies needs and areas for action
- Directs design attention to desired consequences
- Reviews public policy as applied, not just as stated
- Directs attention to the most significant questions
- Encourages a policy perspective based on citizens and society
- Uses retrospective consequences to shape prospective consequences

Plenary Review uses an assessment of consequences to broaden analysis, base review in experience and focus on desirable ends. Review begins with an assessment of past consequences and ends with a selection of desired prospective consequences. Values and end purposes can best be judged on the basis of consequences. Table 3-1 illustrates how the assessment of consequences affects Plenary Review.

The regular review of policy arenas is critical in animating and guiding policy review. The influence of this element in a Plenary Review system is identified in Table 3-2.

TABLE 3–2
INFLUENCE OF PERIODIC REVIEW

**Periodic Review Contributes
to Plenary Review Because It:**

- Enables repeated evaluations and adjustments
- Facilitates the policy agenda and focusing of effort
- Monitors policy impact and developments in the context
- Indicates appropriate times for action
- Identifies needs often unrecognized and averts crisis reaction
- Establishes the long-range view
- Provides insight into cycles of change and adaptation
- Enables regular feedback on system operation

CONTRIBUTIONS TO POLICY DECISIONS

The step up from policies and programs to macro-policy and policy arenas is designed to change the perspective of policy reviews. Thinking must rise to identify and deal with the level of challenges facing the polity. The impact of the broader perspective is presented in Table 3-3.

TABLE 3–3
INFLUENCE OF MACRO–POLICY AND BROADER PERSPECTIVE

The Broader Perspective Contributes to Plenary Review Because It:

- Provides an orientation often missing in policy details and particular programs
- Encourages coherence and consistency in policy arenas
- Identifies policies and programs working at cross-purposes
- Provides perspective to requisite actions
- Encourages a leadership overview
- Informs judgements on subsequent policies and actions
- Encourages review of neglected policy areas
- Enables thinking at the levels appropriate to policy challenges
- Encourages consideration of norms and guiding principles
- Provides the framework and criteria for oversight

The broader perspective expands policy review vertically by raising it to the macro-policy level. The Plenary Review element of more integrated and cohesive policy is intended to broaden review horizontally to consider related policies and programs in a policy arena. Table 3-4 identifies the transforming influence of this Plenary Review element.

TABLE 3–4
INFLUENCE OF MORE INTEGRATED AND COHESIVE POLICY

More Integrated and Cohesive Policy Contributes to Plenary Review Because It:

- Enables comparison in a policy arena
- Provides an evaluative framework for public policy
- Identifies interacting policy influences
- Establishes a broader view
- Notes interaction, competition and complementation of policies
- Enhances desired policy impact
- Encourages policies in needed and neglected areas
- Encourages general macro-policy statements

The guiding direction is designed to guide future actions within each policy arena. The output of a Plenary Review, the guiding direction, will have a continuing influence in steering the public policy body and its governance actions. This influence is listed in Table 3-5.

TABLE 3–5
INFLUENCE OF THE GUIDING DIRECTION

The Guiding Direction Contributes to Plenary Review Because It:

- Provides the basis for coordination of policies
- Establishes evaluative criteria
- Guides rules, regulations and implementing decisions
- Guides strategic actions and adaptation
- Enables consideration of normative and philosophical matters
- Establishes a general policy framework and policy purposes
- Contributes to governance decisions
- Enables adaptation as it and its applications are periodically reviewed and adjusted

In addition to the core elements of Plenary Review, Chapter Two also presented three elements which enhance the Plenary Review decision process. These are also important transforming influences in Plenary Review and its decision process. In the first, Plenary Review is best conducted through a deliberative and participative process. Such a process is designed to fit most policy bodies and to facilitate evaluation and judgement. Table 3-6 identifies the contribution made by a deliberative process.

TABLE 3–6
INFLUENCE OF A
DELIBERATIVE PROCESS

A Deliberative Process Contributes to Plenary Review Because It:
• Facilitates judgement and evaluation
• Encourages creativity and development
• Encourages comparison of options and refinement of alternatives
• Allows representation of views
• Broadens interests and perspectives
• Provides legitimacy

Contributions to Policy Decisions

The requirement for a decision to conclude Plenary Review deliberations is an important influence. It influences the deliberative focus as well as requiring some action. Table 3-7 lists the influences of required decisions.

TABLE 3–7
INFLUENCE OF REQUIREMENT FOR DECISION

The Requirement for Decision Contributes to Plenary Review Because It:
• Forces evaluation and concrete choices
• Directs participants from analysis to action
• Structures attention on practical concerns
• Establishes the best answer possible at that time
• Encourages a forward-looking perspective
• Highlights the actions necessary to desired ends
• Establishes governance decisions
• Reduces avoidance of issues

In Plenary Review, decisions are made by quantitative vote to enable some resolution. Such an approach is also designed to fit the processes of most public policy bodies. Table 3-8 identifies the influence of quantitative resolution.

TABLE 3–8
INFLUENCE OF QUANTITATIVE RESOLUTION

Quantitative Resolution Contributes to Plenary Review Because It:

- Utilizes existing processes of most public policy bodies
- Encourages decision and action or confirmation
- Recognizes need for decision when there is no consensus

In Plenary Review, the decision process is used to uncover and articulate goals and arrive at certain ends. The Plenary Review process is designed to expand thinking, generate more alternatives, expand considerations to include the political, economic, moral, social and institutional consequences, broaden perspectives, encourage action, and assist analysis. The Plenary Review decision process is intended to enable more effective policy decisions. The Plenary Review decision process is not the end, but the means for better policy review and direction. It is a mechanism for the policy body to better carry out its responsibilities.

PLENARY REVIEW AND DECISION MAKING RATIONALITY

Are Plenary Review decisions more rational than the decisions made through other approaches? Would Plenary Review decisions be better or more effective than decisions made in the current public policy process? Is Plenary Review as a separate mode superior to the current public policy and legislative modes? These questions tie into a long debate about decision making processes and their rationality. A brief review of what constitutes rationality sets the stage for a discussion of whether Plenary Review decisions are more rational. The most notable entries in this debate are the synoptic or rational model criticized by Simon (1945), Lindblom's incremental partisan mutual adjustment model (1959), and Etzioni's mixed scanning model (1967 and 1986). These models differ in their conceptualization of the breadth of the decision-makers' definition of a policy problem. As Max Stephenson has pointed out in Plenary Review discussions, these approaches have been helpful in understanding decision making but they offer little guidance for the design of a decision-making process with hopes of improving policy decisions.

The definition of rationality becomes conceptually very important. Although somewhat an academic concern, the problems of defining rationality lead to an important understanding of Plenary Review decisions. In the late 1940's and early 1950's, the so-called rationalist approach to decision making suggested that officials preparing to make a policy choice should seek to identify all relevant courses of action, systematically weigh the advantages and disadvantages of each alternative and choose that path which maximized the relevant aims or values of the decision maker or organization. In short, in this view, policy makers who aspire to rationality must somehow develop the capacity to identify all possible alternative strategies, determine the consequences that follow upon each strategy and systematically compare each set of consequences identified (note Smithies, 1955).

Herbert Simon and Charles Lindblom both argued that the actual practice of administrators facing decisions fell far short of this ideal. Simon suggested that decision-makers' actual behavior varied from the rationalist's tenets in at least three basic ways (Simon, 1945: 81). First, rationality requires a complete knowledge and anticipation of the consequences that follow on each choice. In fact, knowledge of consequences is always fragmentary. Second, since these consequences lie in the future, imagination must supply the lack of experience in attaching value to them. But value can be only imperfectly determined. Third, rationality requires a choice among all possible alternative behaviors. In actual situations, only a very few of all these possible alternatives come to mind. Simon argued that any new approach to understanding decision making should begin by accepting the fact that human beings are capable only of "bounded rationality," that is, circumscribed or limited rationality. The capacity of the human mind is very small compared to the size and complexity of the problems (Simon, 1945: xxiv).

For his part, Lindblom advocated decision making by successive limited comparisons (incrementalism) as a means by which decision makers could realistically overcome their cognitive limitations (1959: 79-88). Lindblom did not chose to question the definition of rationality as an all-encompassing capacity to recognize and consider every possible alternative and every conceivable factor which might somehow be of consequence to the matter under study, at the time of the decision or in the future. Lindblom did not assert that incrementalism was rational; only that it was practical and that it was everywhere employed.

Amitai Etzioni first advanced the concept of "mixed scanning" in 1967 arguing that context-setting decisions set the framework in which incremental choices are later made (1967: 385-392). For him, mixed scanning was a hierarchical mode of decision making that combined higher order, fundamental decisions with lower order, incremental decisions that work out and/or prepare for the higher order ones (Etzioni, 1986: 8-14). Etzioni, however, also accepted a definition of rationality as an all-encompassing capacity to recognize and evaluate all relevant alternatives.

Mixed scanning, incrementalism and rationalism all accepted a particular definition of rational action as omniscient or fully knowing action. Despite their significant differences in approach, all three major models of policy decision-making shared a common conception of rationality. The limitation (boundedness) of rationality is a major conceptual problem with which many have attempted to deal in different ways (Forester, 1984: 23-31). Given rationality as knowing action, few could be said ever to chose in a rational way. And no practicing legislator, executive or administrator dealing with complex questions of public policy has ever approached rationality, much less achieved it, no matter now Herculean the effort. All major approaches deny the possibility of completely rational action out of hand since each imposes upon the decision maker an unlimited responsibility. This definition of rationality confronts the decision maker with an unsolvable dilemma. Attempts to approximate rationality will lead to endless analyses of possibly or potentially relevant factors and consequences, resulting in an inability to act. But an unwillingness to act is, in principle, irrational and irresponsible. Such a conception of rationality—as reflected in decades of discussion in the literature—condemns all legislative, executive and administrative action, at worst, to the realm of irrationality, and at best to the sphere of partial or incomplete rationality.

Since legislators and administrators must make decisions daily, it appears that they must "satisfice," that is, attempt to select that which will suffice and will satisfy requirements. Unfortunately this concept, coined by Simon, provides little or no guidance to responsible officials as they go about the process of weighing the conflicting values which are necessarily the province of decisions. Somewhere, somehow, responsible officials do in fact assign weights to values either consciously or by implication. Simply suggesting that these choice processes fall short of one conception of rationality is of little use or consequence to a beleaguered decision maker. Surely, whatever the label assigned to their actions, legislators, policy makers and administrators have always sought to adopt courses of action which are sufficient to meet the exigencies of the circumstances in which they find themselves.

This somewhat academic background now provides the basis for discussing Plenary Review decisions. Plenary Review rejects the notion of bounded rationality and the definition from which it arises, accepting in its stead the view that a decision-maker's responsibility is limited to the courses of action that would have been considered and the consequences that could have been foreseen by a reasonable individual or body at the time of decision. In this view, it is enough that policy makers consider as many courses of action as time, knowledge and circumstances permit, responding to the comprehensive questions of moral, economic, political and social consequences, taking the best available appropriate action (quantitatively determined by vote) at that time, and adapting as the process continues in the future. This is acting as best and humanly possible. Such an effort would constitute a rational course in the context which confronted the decision maker. Plenary Review, thus, does not rely upon an abstract model of rationality but rather determines general rationality in the context of specific policy actions and circumstances. Plenary Review will have to be assessed as a practical decision process useful in a variety of contexts with the goal of enabling more thoughtful and effective collective decisions, stated in general guiding terms.

Plenary Review does not seek some absolute kind of rationality. It seeks reasonableness and adaptation within the given context. Rather than agonize about dilemmas of rationality, Plenary Review attempts to meet challenges in review and action as best possible, not "right" but "best." Moreover, Plenary Review provides decision makers with a focus and format by which to prepare and make actual policy choices. Rather than lament the incapacity of policy makers to behave rationally, the Plenary Review process provides them with a perspective through which to consider existing policy and its interpreting implementation in a thoroughgoing and systematic way. The approach is both rooted in the reality of a policy makers's everyday needs and is modestly pragmatic about how best to serve those requirements.

Neither Plenary Review nor any other decision format can insure the "best" decision. Plenary Review simply attempts to facilitate the "best available" decision which can be made through always limited information and responsible decision makers at a particular time. Attempting to evaluate the policy consequences, discern future needs and establish general guiding purposes will be better than not doing so. It is also important to recognize that Plenary Review does not result in a final decision on guiding direction which must be perfect in that iteration. Since periodic assessment is central to the Plenary Review concept, each decision will again be reviewed in a few years and adjustments made with the best attainable decision at that time. This cycle will be repeated again and again as new insights and circumstances warrant. The policy body will regularly review the consequences of the various specific policies and programs, generalize to establish a guiding direction, review consequences and modify the guiding direction. Were Plenary Review used in the national legislature, for example, Congress would simply deliberate on a particular policy arena and decide by vote on a guiding direction as best it can; it would then review that decision and its consequences after a number of years in order to develop adjustments to it.

Plenary Review does not propose a narrow technique which carefully follows the steps of decision making to a predetermined end. Policy challenges do not lend themselves to such a limited approach and policy bodies must respond beyond technical designs. In more recent work, Etzioni has argued that because of the challenges, "decision making in the 1990's will be even more of an art and less of a science than it is today" (Etzioni, 1989: 122). Current decisionmaking approaches are often inadequate, he maintained, and demands of information, time, and context are forcing what he termed "humble decision making." This approach recognizes the challenges and the need to decide and adapt as best one can. He noted several essential qualities for decision making in today's world: flexibility, caution and the capacity to proceed with partial knowledge. He concluded that "Only fools make rigid decisions and decisions with no sense of overarching purpose" (1989: 126). Plenary Review also argues that decision makers must proceed as best possible to meet the challenges. Imperfection of process or outcome does not warrant avoiding the effort.

Interaction of Viewpoints

If Plenary Review does not guarantee a perfect or best decision, how can we rely on it to make such important macro-policy decisions and to provide guiding direction for a democracy? Of course, this is essentially the same issue as the longstanding debate over majority rule. It can not be logically shown that the majority will always, or even usually, be "right" (Riker, 1988). The proposition can still be made—even though not capable of logical proof—that majorities somehow will tend to make better decisions. Although logic can not show that Plenary Review will assure better decisions, the proposition is asserted here—for judgement, rather than strict logic—that a focus on consequences and a determination of guiding direction will enable a policy body to respond much more effectively to the sequence of challenges which it will always face. Plenary Review will contribute to the decision making of policy bodies in a major way because it raises important perspectives and issues not currently well considered and it encourages coherence and consistency in an interactive process not often found in current policy processes. And, Plenary Review will focus on larger issues, such as values and ends, not adequately considered in current policy making.

How are agreement and disagreement handled in Plenary Review discussions and conclusions? There is no presumption that full consensus will be achieved in the formulation of the Plenary Review guiding direction. Of course, consensus can occur, since general agreement on goals often can be easier than agreement on specifics. However, conflict, contrasting viewpoints, contradictory attitudes and opposing interests will be part of Plenary Review discussions. The variety of viewpoints and value judgements in a policy body (as in their current policy decisions) will not be radically different in a Plenary Review format. There will seldom be radical changes from existing viewpoints and coalitions in Congress or other policy bodies operating in a Plenary Review mode. Such diversity is accepted and used to enhance deliberations. Decisions are possible in the Plenary Review mode because they are made quantitatively by majority vote (as is currently the case in the regular policy mode).

For example, effective congressional decision making does not require fully rational objectivity or complete consensus of view. As Kingdon has contended with respect to useable information, subjective evaluations are often more useable than objective stances (1973: 219-220). Although some observers call for "neutral" information (that which is not "tainted" by vested interest or bias), Kingdon has argued that such information often is less useful than information which takes a position and buttresses its argument with selected facts. "This is true," he says, "because evaluative information is of necessity directly focused on the issue at hand." Debates can be enhanced and their resulting decisions improved through competition of viewpoint and information. To use an illustration at the federal level, Plenary Review rests not on the development of a consensus leading to action any more than consensus is required in current congressional discussions and decisions. Since the Plenary Review mode will continue in successive iterations, the debates will continue as Congress attempts to confront significant issues in the designated policy arenas.

Discussion and decision in Plenary Review will be influenced by all the factors currently influencing Congress. Established issue networks will continue to be an important influence on congressional decision-making (Heclo, 1978: 116). Party, ideology, the characteristics of participants, past actions and evolution of the issues (Asher & Weisberg, 1985: 427-428) will also be at work in the Plenary Review mode of congressional deliberations. Decision outcomes in Congress will continue to be influenced by the organizational hierarchy, by the voting system and by bargaining and interaction. Interaction and cues from other congressmen will continue greatly to influence congressional decision making (Matthews & Stimson, 1975: 77). Congressional decision making in the Plenary Review mode will likewise be influenced by information flow and by the progressive narrowing of alternatives (Kingdon, 1973: 215-231, 270). Plenary Review will have to work in the legislative culture of decentralization and fragmentation. While congressional reform might be both possible and desirable, Plenary Review does not rest on reform of congressional structure, process or motivation.

Plenary Review does not assume that a "body of angels" will sit to establish guiding purposes; there will be disagreements and conflicting viewpoints. Plenary Review will work within the existing structure, influences, motivations and participants of the policy body. At the same time, of course, Plenary Review adds a separate mode of deliberation and decision at the macro-policy level which will add its own influence to the existing process. Plenary Review does not depend on consensus or agreement, but is designed to operate in the rich mix of viewpoints and values.

SUMMARY

Plenary Review is a complementary decision process for use by bodies with public policy responsibilities. A prime application of this decision process would be as a second decision mode in the United States Congress. While Plenary Review considers macro-policy concerns and guiding purposes, it is grounded in the practical and the applied in its assessment of consequences and prospective policy guidance.

The core elements of Plenary Review exert a transforming influence on the decision process. The Plenary Review characteristic elements influence policy decisions by stimulating certain perspectives, enabling beneficial insights, encouraging deliberative actions and informing outcomes. They are elements which will flavor and shape the policy process toward meeting the needs and challenges which are ever unfolding. Plenary Review is not designed as a decision technique, but rather as a structuring influence which will enable policy bodies to better assess past policies and direct future actions.

Plenary Review does not rely on an abstract model of rationality to argue that it is a superior process or that its decisions are better. Rather, Plenary Review expects only the improvement of decisions, as best possible in a given context. Plenary Review accepts the imperfection of any decision or process and is designed to regularly re-visit and re-adjust all public policy decisions as assessment of consequences and additional insight make possible.

Four: Plenary Review as Governance

Plenary Review is policy making at the level of governance. Plenary Review assesses the consequences of specific policies and programs to develop general guiding directions. This Chapter will discuss Plenary Review as macro-policy important in governance of the polity. The stage is set, first, by reviewing the substantial concerns about the Constitution and the numerous calls for constitutional revision. Second, the charges of congressional ineffectiveness and the calls for congressional reform will be noted. These will lead to a discussion of Plenary Review as a governance level macro-policy mode through which the effectiveness of Congress and the constitutional system might be improved.

Concerns for Constitutional Revision

The Constitution of the United States establishes the framework of government and expresses the principles upon which the polity operates. Although the Constitution has been nothing short of remarkable in providing guidance for two hundred years, there are many who are concerned about its continued effectiveness and many who have called for reform of the constitutional system. The concern about the Constitution buttresses the point that consideration should be given to concepts—such as Plenary Review—which may be able to make a contribution in meeting these concerns.

The Constitution has been a challenge to operate. Before the turn of the last century, Woodrow Wilson noted that the challenge had become to learn how "to run a constitution" (Stillman, 1988: 813). Even then, Wilson questioned "whether the Constitution is still adapted to serve the purposes for which it was intended" and he observed that there has been "a vast alteration in the conditions of government" (Eidelberg, 1974: 279). More recently, James MacGregor Burns concluded that to deal with some problems in the governmental system "we must directly confront the constitutional structure" erected by the Founders (1984: 189).

The literature calling for constitutional reform is extensive. General works calling for significant constitutional changes include William MacDonald, *A New Constitution for America* (1921), William Yandell Elliott, *The Need for Constitutional Reform* (1935), Henry Hazlitt, *A New Constitution Now* (1942), Charles M. Hardin, *Presidential Power and Accountability: Toward a New Constitution* (1974) and Rexford G. Tugwell, *A Model Constitution for a United Republics of America* (1976).

The most recent call for constitutional reform is illustrative of abiding concerns. The Committee on the Constitutional System, which includes many prominent individuals from recent Democratic and Republican Administrations, has added a plea for targeted change in the Constitution (Brookings, 1987). Lloyd Cutler, the founder and co-chair of the Committee on the Constitutional System, contended that over the last fifty years "massive failures have developed in the sum of the results, the sum of the outcomes that the federal government is achieving" (Brookings, 1987: 1). The Committee then called for constitutional reform, particularly to create responsible leadership and reduce deadlock in the separation of powers. The proposals are presented as a *Government for the Third American Century* (Robinson, 1989).

James Sundquist has reviewed an extensive list of needs and reform proposals in *Constitutional Reform and Effective Government* (1986). The chapter headings of his major work on the subject suggest the issues: forestalling divided government, lengthening terms of office, reconstituting a failed government, fostering interbranch collaboration and altering checks and balances (1986: 75-238). He concluded his survey of major arguments for reform by observing that many experienced leaders who are advocating constitutional revision are "profoundly convinced that the United States has been lucky in the past and that, in the future, the deadlock and indecision built into the governmental structure will place the nation in continued peril" (1986: 239). He argued that there have been enough periods of governmental failure in the nation's past to suggest the need to identify weaknesses and adopt remedies.

To buttress his argument for substantial revision in the Constitution, Rexford Tugwell pointed to the provisions which are no longer relevant, such as quartering soldiers in citizen's houses and using twenty dollars as the dividing line between jury and non-jury trials. He also argued that changing circumstances have undermined the rationale for many provisions, such as the terms for national officials (designed for selectmen of the 1780s rather than a national electorate) and the number in the Senate from each state (designed to conciliate antiunionist politicians). He noted the lack of provisions for education, health, the economy or an industrial society (Tugwell, 1976: 7-10). He concluded that since much of the initial Constitution has disappeared through reinterpretation and since it is desirable to have a constitution, then "a careful but complete recasting is indicated" (1976: 172). The logic for a revised constitution, Tugwell argued, is irrefutable (1976: 6-7). If the Constitution were submitted to referendum now, the *literal* Constitution would not be ratified. If not, and if constitutional government is desirable, he maintained, then it follows that a revised constitution ought to be devised.

The calls for constitutional revision evidence a widespread concern for the ability of the Constitution to meet current challenges. Since the processes which allow the Constitution to adapt and meet current needs while maintaining the basic framework are crucial, approaches which facilitate this adaptation (such as Plenary Review) are clearly worthy of serious consideration. Since the Constitution does not attempt to provide a substantive macro-policy framework—the policy gap discussed in Chapter One, approaches (such as Plenary Review) which encourage more coherent and integrated policy may prove important supplements to the constitutional framework. Since constitutional interpretation is important to public policy, approaches (such as Plenary Review) which would facilitate analysis, deliberation and decision are important to assess.

CONCERNS FOR CONSTITUTIONAL REFORM

Both those who participate in and those who study legislatures have been greatly concerned about legislative effectiveness. David Truman once observed that "the twentieth century has been hard on legislatures" (1959: 1) and he was only reviewing the first half. Congress and other legislatures have had a difficult time measuring up to the demands and challenges of the society and political system. The result is that by whatever evaluative criteria, critics of all persuasions have found Congress wanting (Rieselbach, 1977: 33). Some concerns for congressional reform will be reviewed in this section because they justify the consideration of concepts—such as Plenary Review—which address these concerns.

The literature on congressional reform is nearly overwhelming in its size and scope. One student of the institution has suggested that the "genre is apparently inexhaustible" (Polsby, 1986: 202). In 1963, for example, the *Congressional Quarterly* listed criticisms of and proposals for reform of Congress. It took 62 double-column pages just to list congressional problems and reform proposals (Huitt, 1965: 98-101). A recent search of the Congressional Research Service Bibliographic Data Base listed 129 citations between 1969 and 1985 on congressional reform conducted just by congressional bodies. The titles of a few reform-oriented books are illustrative of the concern: Congress is "on trial," a sink of "corruption and compromise," responsible for the "deadlock of democracy," and a "sapless branch" of government. Similarly, the body is "in crisis" and may be described as a "house out of order." "Congress," according to another author, "needs help." Bert Gross once entitled an article "Toward a House of Worse Repute or How to Be a Rubber Stamp with Honor" (1973: 767-783).

The criticism of Congress spans the history of the institution. Late in the nineteenth century, Woodrow Wilson wrote one of the first important books on the subject of congressional effectiveness. Although Congress should lead the nation to its "conclusions," to "utter the voice of its opinions, and to serve as its eyes in superintending all matters of government," he concluded that this "Congress does not do" (1885: 195). More recently, Senator Joseph Clark, who was engaged in many reform efforts, spoke for many other Senators and Representatives when he said: "As a working member of Congress, I am a firm believer in the need for congressional reform" (Clark, 1965:

v-vi). It was Clark's opinion that Congress did not require more capable politicians; rather, the cause of ineffectiveness was to be found in the structure and process of Congress. In 1991, Senators David Boren and Pete Dominici and Representatives Lee Hamilton and Willis Gradison proposed the creation of a joint committee to reform Congress (*Washington Post*. 1991). Senator Boren stated that "Congress is bogged down in a morass of detail, missing the big picture and slow to respond to our real problems."

It has been argued that Congress is "seriously flawed as a policy-making instrument" because societal problems are not being well addressed (Davidson & Oleszek, 1977: x). Jones and Marini argued in *The Imperial Congress* that Congress seldom debates the fundamental questions that face the country (1988: 1). Norman Ornstein described it as passive-aggressive politics—avoiding blame and risk (1990: 43). Heineman argued that institutional reform could enhance the effectiveness of policy analysis (1970: 170). Ladd noted that the debate over institutional reform focuses on Congress because it is the branch seen to be working most poorly (1990: 57; see Uslaner, 1990: 492-494). Rexford Tugwell, who has been very much involved in the study of government and presidential administration from the New Deal to current times, has observed that "to reform the legislature has always been the most obvious way to better government" (Tugwell, 1970: 36). But Tugwell has also argued that it has been the one reform about which nothing substantial has been done. In an American Assembly volume on Congress, David Truman commented that "unless ways are found to alter the functioning of Congress, the fortunes of the nation may be inadequately guarded or seriously diminished" (Truman, 1965: 1). Michael Mezey has argued that the "Congress seems structurally incapable of producing public policy that is informed, timely, coherent, effective and responsible" (1989: 142-143).

There is substantial disagreement and uncertainty even about what function Congress should perform for the polity. Without ascertaining the function, it is not possible to evaluate Congress fully (Davidson & Oleszek, 1977: 3). If we evaluate Congress for responsibility, we will focus on problem solving; if we evaluate Congress for responsiveness, we may focus more on process than product; if we evaluate Congress for accountability, we must consider the electorate (Rieselbach, 1977: 8-9). Reviewing various functions, Shepsle has argued that Congress articulates interests superbly, but aggregates them poorly (1988: 464).

While there are many critics, there are also those who defend Congress. Patterson, for example, compares various national representative assemblies and concludes that "the American Congress continues to be a significant, independent, lawmaking institution, capable of legislative innovation and able to undertake the creative act of lawmaking without executive leadership if necessary" (1978: 125). Rieselbach has argued that Congress still possesses the constitutional and statutory means to have a significant impact on the formation of public policy (Rieselbach, 1977: 3). Polsby said that "there is something uncivil" about insisting on constitutional reforms to cure political ailments (1990: 17). And a number of authors in a volume on congressional leadership sponsored by the Dirksen Congressional Center argued that leadership is still possible (Kornacki, 1990). The *Journal of Public Policy and Management* included a symposium to investigate why the American political system, which is usually in gridlock and paralysis, has been capable of action on some major issues (Melnick, 1991).

The concerns which have been reviewed should not be taken to mean that Congress has not changed or that it has not instituted reforms. As one would expect, Congress has changed and adapted in response to both reform attempts and external forces. In his research on congressional floor policy making, Smith reported institutional innovation and adaptation to changing conditions (1989: 233). Many changes have strengthened the Congress relative to the Presidency, opened the institution to more public scrutiny and dispersed power within the body more widely (Parker, 1985: 482-483). Reforms of the committee system and party leadership have been attempted (Ornstein, 1975: 262-264). Rieselbach reviewed a wide variety of reform proposals (1973: 365-388) and concluded that reforms further diffused authority even while congressional power with respect to the presidency was being reasserted (1977: 42). Shepsle has listed reduction of disparities among committees, enlargement and wider distribution of member resources, taming of former power centers, sunshine reforms, reassertion of legislative branch powers, centralization of legislative parties and curbing of minority obstruction as the major reforms of the 1970's (1988: 462). Important congressional changes have included more democratic procedures, revived party caucuses, a new congressional budget control system and changes in committee and subcommittee chairmanship selection procedures (Oleszek, 1984: 36-39). In sum, James MacGregor Burns has argued that the reforms achieved in the past two or three decades show Congress to have "an impressive capacity to reorder its internal power structure" (1984: 175).

The changes illustrate that Congress is not immune to either social forces or internal pressures (Shepsle, 1988: 461). Adaptive change often seems to come slowly, but over time it can be readily observed in the Congress. Adaptive change has occurred in response to external demands, such as a major crisis or catastrophe. It has come from internal tensions, cycles of leadership centralization and dispersion, and tension between the executive and the legislature (Patterson, 1978: 133-135). None of this is to say that reform is easy or consensual. Although it is stimulated by events and crises, reform is difficult to achieve (Davidson, 1966: 66). Perhaps the difficulty of reform is well summarized by the response of Senator Everett Dirksen to a proposal for change. He is reported to have said, "ha, ha, ha, and I might add: ho, ho, ho" (Davidson, 1966: 78-79).

The difficulty of change is greatly increased by the trade-offs which characterize most choices. For example, if the standing committees are made more representative or more responsive to majoritarian preferences this may at the same time diminish the division of labor, reduce the career attractiveness of the legislature, and make the legislature more permeable to outside forces, such as the executive (Shepsle, 1988: 475). One can also argue that many of the changes to improve efficiency and decision making are dysfunctional for the deliberative and political functions of Congress.

Since there is concern about congressional effectiveness, and since there are calls for congressional reform, then concepts and processes which address these concerns—such as Plenary Review—merit consideration. And proposals—such as Plenary Review—which are on-going adaptive responses rather than one-shot modifications, are particularly important to evaluate.

GOVERNANCE
POLICY REVIEW

Lawmakers, the public and policy analysts alike share an abiding concern for effective public policy, and there have been countless debates over various policies. While concern for particular public policies is necessary and beneficial, there also needs to be effective review of public policy at a higher level of generality—at the level of governance. Plenary Review deals directly with these questions of purpose, direction and developing outcomes—the significant issues about governance and the determination of the public interest at the level of the polity. Plenary Review functions as a higher-level complement to guide and inform the regular policy process (which generally and even necessarily focuses on the particulars). Plenary Review is governance level policy review and action in a policy body. The following sections will discuss Plenary Review as governance.

There is grave concern in many quarters about governance level challenges. Three examples may illustrate this concern. The Governance Project at the Center for National Policy recently published a report entitled *America Tomorrow: The Choices We Face* (Steinbruner, 1989). The report is concerned with what the polity will be tomorrow, where it is heading, and what the central choices are which we face. And *Time* magazine ran a cover story asking, "Is Government Dead?" (*Time*, October 23, 1989). The story was distressed with the inability of political leaders to determine direction, make choices and confront needs. Illustrated by a cover picture showing George Washington with a tear, *Time* argued that America was slipping into paralysis. And after reviewing symposium papers on the "new politics of public policy," Ellwood concludes that "what is needed, therefore, is political action in the tradition of the founding fathers. Such action is in the arena of politics writ large rather than the professional expert" (Ellwood, 1991).

A fundamental challenge, particularly in a democracy, is to take actions and find institutional arrangements which will produce public policy that will meet the long-term needs of the system. The challenge is not just for effective individual public policies at the level or responsibility of the policy body (e.g., statutory law, policy statement), but that these policies all fit together, that they move in the democratically desired direction and that they meet governance level concerns.

Table 4-1 shows how the elements of Plenary Review raise review to the level of governance decisions.

Plenary Review particularly complements governance concerns through its ability to recognize and debate cross-cutting issues which may not adequately surface in the focus on individual policies. For example, cross-cutting issues might include the appropriate degree of centralization or decentralization, the subsequent degree of judicial interpretation which is beneficial, the impact of policy actions on the family, legitimacy, justice and so forth. These broader aspects are not effectively recognized because the debates in most public policy bodies are necessarily geared to the details. These cross-cutting issues deal with general results rather than specifications in the detailed language of the necessary enactments. Enactment is specific, directive, corrective and mandating. There is a need also for regular deliberation of that which is directional, integrative, philosophical and related to basic frameworks and purposes of governance.

TABLE 4–1
PLENARY REVIEW
AND GOVERNANCE

The elements of Plenary Review raise the policy focus to the governance level:
• The assessment of social, economic, moral, political and institutional consequences raises the level of generality and confronts basic issues.
• The periodic review adds a separate mode by which major policy arenas are regularly evaluated.
• The perspective of macro-policy encourages a broad and long-term perspective and raises the level of generality.
• More coherent and integrated policy extends effective review to include related programs and policies and broadens the scope.
• The guiding direction establishes public purposes and desirable future states, itself subject to regular review.

As was the case in the Byzantine empire, ancient China and other historical periods, there can be effective administration without the larger perspective and understanding of adaptive direction which democratic governance does require. Policy enactment and administration may be internally consistent but lack understanding of the larger framework and results. Rather than always grinding finer in the policy process, we need to understand governance and developing purposes.

Governance level review can be further illustrated with a related notion. In the legal system, the concept of due process has been an essential criterion for court review. Legal interpretation has had to distinguish between procedural due process and substantive due process. It is interesting to speculate how things might be different today had the U.S. Supreme Court not ultimately abandoned substantive due process (Thompson, 1989: 493). In similar ways, Plenary Review touches on substantive due process notions. That is, policy enactments, rules and regulations would be issued within and be interpreted from some developing determination of valid purposes and desirable outcomes. As with substantive due process, Plenary Review would be an attempt to develop guidelines over time to direct individual policy enactments. There is no expectation that all such issues will be easily or finally determined or that they will remain unchanged even when specified. The expectation only is that these guiding purposes are considered and that they inform specific policy actions as they develop over time.

Plenary Review is a complementary format that will provide insight and understanding through grappling with substantive governance level questions. Using the national legislature as an example for policy bodies, the current pair of congressional eye glasses may enable it to see matters up close, but another prescription may be needed to see more broadly. Or, in another simile, Plenary Review intends that Congress be able to diagnose and understand before it prescribes.

Plenary Review and Government Control

In its broad perspective and concern for macro-policy, Plenary Review can be used to address some very important questions about the role of the state, the relationship of the individual to government and the debate between free market and centralized control. This raises questions about Plenary Review itself. Does Plenary Review encourage centralized control and a greatly increased level of government direction? Is Plenary Review democratic planning? Is Plenary Review liberal or conservative in its impact?

These questions about the impact of Plenary Review are very significant because they deal with the basic role of government and its relationship to its citizens. As applied to the U.S. government and Congress, some assume that Plenary Review is liberal in its impact because it appears to expand the role of the state. This is not necessarily so; it can either expand or contract the role of the State. Plenary Review does not have to be either conservative or liberal. Indeed, Plenary Review decisions could be from time to time, either liberal or conservative in their effect. And Plenary Review can have either a centralizing or decentralizing influence depending on the actual deliberations and decisions. Further responses to these concerns can be grouped in three categories. First, Plenary Review is a structural middle ground in the debate over the degree of control. Second, Plenary Review is itself an effective mechanism to address periodically the question of the proper balance. Third, Plenary Review enriches the debate over the balance through periodic review of fundamental concerns.

Plenary Review as Structural Middle Ground

The longstanding debate over the relationship of the individual and the governing collective is not one which Plenary Review will resolve. Questions about individual responsibility and collective needs will continue to invigorate discussions of socialism versus the free market, communism versus capitalism and the rights of the individual versus the rights and power of the aggregate. As in the past, some will trust the free market, the invisible hand, to work out many matters of public concern; others will call for democratic planning and a substantial degree of collective regulation to insure the public good.

In a limited way, Plenary Review may be considered to be a structural middle ground between these classic positions. As a format or process, Plenary Review does not attempt to specify the details and plan the particulars. On the other hand, it does attempt to give general direction and influence the collective. Plenary Review could be used to inform the consequent policy actions where democratic planning is seen to be needed. It could also serve to stimulate debate and insight into general societal trends, resulting in a contraction or expansion of the governance functions from time to time.

Plenary Review statements of guiding direction should not be taken to be a comprehensive plan. It is important to distinguish between aggregating the particulars and establishing a separate level of governance review. There is a large literature which argues that governments are not able to consider all the interdependencies and choices in decisions (see Kingdon, 1984, and Steinbruner, 1974). Those who have studied strategic change argue that "decisions do not lend themselves to aggregation into a single massive decision matrix where all factors can be treated relatively simultaneously in order to arrive at a holistic optimum" (Quinn, 1989: 53). Recent experience in the USSR validates this point. Plenary Review *does not* intend to create a comprehensive system which builds all specific policy choices and programs into one coordinated whole. This would be virtually impossible to orchestrate and would not be desirable in its centrally determined outcome. Rather, Plenary Review simply attempts to institute a separate process of review in which general governance questions can be deliberated and determined. That determination—the statement of guiding purposes and direction—insures that important questions are considered. A policy body will sooner or later have to struggle with these larger issues in some fashion—often merely haphazard, defensive or declarative. Under the Plenary Review concept, specific policy enactments would have to refer to these general statements, but current action would not be constrained in changing them.

As a structural system, Plenary Review is neither a centralized coordinating mechanism nor a laissez-faire free market. It is a structural middle ground which attempts regularly to coordinate and inform through deliberation of general goals and governance needs.

Plenary Review Addressing the Balance

There are important rationales and supporting warrants for each position in the perpetual governance debate between the individual and the collective. The answers are usually balances and tradeoffs between the two extremes. How much control and regulation is appropriate at any particular time? How best can individual rights and freedoms be balanced against collective needs? Are the times appropriate for even more regulation or for systematic de-regulation in a particular policy arena? Where should the balance lie at any one time in a particular policy arena? These are exactly the kinds of significant question which Plenary Review considers and decides for the present moment and the immediate future in separate policy arenas, with regular review and adjusting revisions at definite future intervals. Plenary Review considers specifically what the consequences have been, what the balance now should be, and what discrete consequences should be sought in each of the various arenas of public policy.

Plenary Review debate would consider the advantages of utilizing the free market, with its myriad individual decision makers acting effectively upon their individual judgements, but it would also recognize the current limits which would be most appropriate for the collective public interest. Plenary Review does not assume that its answers to such questions are or can be determinative for all future time. There are no final answers to such questions as these, as the entire history of philosophy and of political science so clearly records. Plenary Review attempts, very practically, to give these eternally significant questions the best debate and the best judgement available at that time to the responsible organizations of governance. These questions and their deliberative evaluations, after a period of application and experience, are again reviewed and adaptively revised at regular intervals. The focus of Plenary Review on public policies will inherently bring forward the significant questions of the best current balances between the individual and the state, or the free market and collective regulations.

Plenary Review Adds to the Debate

The struggle between the individual and the collective is usually debated in economic terms. Many political systems are defined by economic concepts and operations, such as capitalism and socialism. It does not detract from these important matters to add other concerns and consequences which are also significant. Plenary Review attempts to bring into focus the social, moral, political and institutional as well as economic consequences. In its focus on past and prospective consequences, Plenary Review helps greatly to enrich and inform the debate about the balance between centralized control and individual rights of action. It can never finally resolve these questions, but Plenary Review will improve the deliberative discussions and public policy decisions through inclusion of these broader concerns.

GOVERNANCE ACTION IN A PLURALISTIC PROCESS

Many have faith that the myriad decisions of free markets result in the most beneficial consequences and decisions for the collective. In this view, the myriad of individual decisions aggregate almost ineluctably for the benefit of the whole, whether such be their individual intentions or not. In the realm of politics and governance, there exists a similar philosophy. Many have faith that the results of the democratic, pluralistic system are beneficial for the collective, provided only reasonably wide limits or boundaries are preserved. The myriad of individual and group interactions are seen to aggregate to the cumulative benefit of the whole. Out of these views rises an important issue related to governance and Plenary Review. Some would argue that the pluralistic group interplay results in a nicely balanced system which operates quite well at present. The system, while not known for its speed and innovation, does provide a check and balance which prepares and refines policy initiatives. The argument can be taken further to contend that a great strength of the present system is that it is inherently ambiguous and unclear, and thus allows scope for and encourages individual initiatives and useful actions. This allows disparate groups to come together in building coalitions of support adequate to make decisions and enact policies. Logical and prescriptive clarity would, under this argument, sharpen the unavoidable pluralistic differences and impede the development of consensus and adjustment. Ambiguity, such an argument maintains, is basic to democratic flexibility and adjustment.

While it utilizes (and does not seek to change) the pluralistic political interplay, Plenary Review reflects a contrasting philosophy with respect to the advantages of ambiguity. Plenary Review raises significant questions and encourages debate on exactly the kinds of issues which separate individuals and groups—moral, economic, political, social and institutional consequences. While there may be advantages to ambiguity in some policy issues from time to time, there can also be advantages to sharpening the debate and consciously putting the best collective efforts into choices of policy direction. Plenary Review reflects an optimistic viewpoint that the collective ought to and is able to make wise and useful judgements and assumes that all significant matters should not be left to an unguided process. While the pluralistic political process, group interests and partisan mutual adjustment work wonderfully well in many cases, these are not always adequate to provide the coordination, coherence, integration and leadership which are often required to meet growing or immediate challenges.

To borrow from the economic analogy, the "invisible hand" of pluralistic interplay in the political arena makes many of the numerous decisions which need to be made. The myriad of decisions, actions and influence from a wide variety of groups and individuals can and does result in a self-adjusting and responsive system. Plenary Review does not intend to make all these particular decisions in any event. It *does not* propose to replace this process even if it could. It *does* attempt to *add* a process of conscious deliberation and appropriate action to assess this process and its outcomes and make, timely and appropriate adjustments. While Adam Smith's "invisible hand" does play a real part in the political system, it is also possible, to use Milton Friedman's term, that the "invisible foot" also can stamp out other needed actions. Plenary Review adds to the basic pluralistic process an element of periodic assessment to guide the hand and redirect the foot in necessary cases. No attempt is made to replace the pluralistic group interplay and its role in the numerous decisions which are and must be made. Plenary Review is simply a conscious effort to thoughtfully try to foresee where the interplay has been going and will be going and to make corrections in direction as considered wise and useful.

THE RISKS OF PLENARY REVIEW

The discussion about governance level policy review—the conscious effort of Plenary Review to guide the system—leads to an important question about the risk inherent in tinkering with a governance or policy system. The issue is simple: The status quo is known; the Plenary Review process is unknown and, therefore, risky. Others might cite the aphorism: "If it ain't broke, don't fix it."

An important matter to consider in implementing Plenary Review is the adaptive nature of the concept. Were Plenary Review the kind of proposal which would be "plugged in" and would either "work or blow a fuse," then risks would be substantial. The nature of Plenary Review is quite different, both in development and in operation. The nature of Plenary Review is self-reflection and self-adjustment, assessing what is happening and consciously responding toward that which is desired and thought to be feasible through active deliberations. The risk attached to Plenary Review is also minimized by the fact that it seeks to complement the current policy process rather than replace it. Plenary Review adds an additional perspective which—were it to fail—would still leave the existing process in place.

While some concern over the consequences to the governance system of an untried Plenary Review process is warranted, this concern is kept in perspective by recognizing that all policy making in any policy body is probabilistic—it is the nature of the enterprise. Policy making in the current Congress and other policy bodies—as well as in a Plenary Review policy decision process—is an attempt to change the odds of different possible futures through appropriate intervention. Yehezkel Dror calls this "fuzzy gambling" (1986: 97-99) Since potential benefits are rarely achieved without some risk. Indeed, difficulties and challenges will continue, with or without Plenary Review, although Plenary Review would periodically attempt to assess the consequences and determine adaptive responses.

Since there can be no fully effective method to resolve the risks in an unknown future, a partial response might be fashioned from the conventional wisdom, such as is found in the "Dear Abby" newspaper column. A middle-aged person was concerned about fulfilling the dream of entering medical school because of the age the person would be in ten years when medical education was completed. Abby responded by asking "how old will you be in ten years if you don't go to medical school." If we continue with our present system, in ten years we might be perfectly fine, thank you. But if we give our best effort to identifying and deliberating the moral, social, economic, political and institutional consequences, past and prospective, of major policy areas, developing directions for the actions we feel most appropriate under each Plenary Review, and then periodically taking further readings and making appropriate adjustments, where will be in ten years? We will have some of the same problems we currently have, but we will have given it our best collective effort, and we likely will have anticipated and forestalled some cumulative policy difficulties because we have conscientiously tried to see the broader and longer-term perspective. It also might be worse, either because of Plenary Review guiding directions or in spite of them. If it is worse because nothing was done, Plenary Review, of course, can not be held accountable. If it is worse because of Plenary Review judgements, the remedy is to reassess the situation and take appropriate action.

This remedy—to assess the situation and take appropriate action—is a Plenary Review process solution. In fact, any remedy, save ignoring the problem, is essentially a Plenary Review remedy. The basic Plenary Review notion is deliberate adjustment and adaptation, based on periodic assessment of consequences and desired future directions. Indeed, the basic response to the risk in conducting Plenary Review is that Plenary Review inherently requires periodic evaluation and adjustment. That is, Plenary Review builds in its own corrective device to periodically revisit general policy guidance and make appropriate corrections.

This is not to say that there are not problems of implementation and design in Plenary Review. Much needs to be learned as the concept is applied; experience will lead to important developments and improvements. But the strengths of the process fully deserve to be tested and its weaknesses overcome. Why? Because reasonable persons, in reasonably quiet times, with a reasonable amount of good will can demonstrate yet again that "government of the people, by the people and for the people shall not perish from the earth" and to anticipate times when catastrophe, disintegration or great challenge loom ahead. And while there is risk and uncertainty in any untried and unproven idea, potential benefits must be calculated in judging Plenary Review.

Plenary Review and the Public Interest

Should Plenary Review be adopted? The ultimate test of public policy or of any modification in the governance system—Plenary Review in this case—is largely based on one's conception of the public interest. Although the concept of the public interest has different definitions and is difficult to operationalize, the concept is still helpful in assessing Plenary Review as governance action. A three-part framework (adapted from Glendon Shubert, *The Public Interest*) is employed to provide insight into different assumptions about the public interest and governance level policy review. Although the concepts apply to most policy bodies, the structure provided in the U.S. Constitution will be used to develop the points.

Traditional Constitutional Assumptions

Some people see the governance system rather traditionally and rationally (in that policy is determined by conscious acts). In this view, policy is to be determined by the constitutional branches of government, the executive, legislative and judicial branches. The public interest—effectuated through policy—is enacted by elected representatives and approved by the executive.

Although the public will is enacted through the process specified in the Constitution, some traditionalists assert the legislature as the ultimate determiner of the public interest. They seek to increase legislative power and influence because, in their view, the determination of the collective good is best achieved through the representative assembly. Others prefer leadership through a strong executive. The only official elected by all the people is the President (the Vice President is adjunct to the President); and, the argument goes, presidential leadership is required in these times. A third group would rely on the judiciary as the ultimate protector and interpreter of the public interest.

Individuals with traditional assumptions about the public interest and its determination in the three branches should have little difficulty with the notion of Plenary Review. Plenary Review should simply be seen as a strengthening of the policy deliberation process or as part of the governance responsibility, particularly of the legislature and the executive. More clarity in specifying legislative intent would also assist the judiciary. Plenary Review is closely allied with the traditional and constitutional assumptions about determination of the public interest and governance actions.

Administrative Idealists

Although their assumptions are usually hidden in other trappings, another group of individuals assumes a major role for the administrative agencies and professionals in achieving the public interest. This perspective is usually presented as techniques of policy analysis, planning, program evaluation, efficient management, professional judgement, expertise, advocacy, specialized knowledge and so forth. It is contended that the traditional branches necessarily are both inexpert and ineffective. But in this view, professionals, policy analysts and administrators, knowledgeable in their areas, should advocate policies, guide presidential and congressional actions, add expertise and knowledge, and carry out the public interest by responsible and professional action.

In one variation, the professionals are seen as policy engineers, advocating policy options based on technical expertise and bringing the political and administrative processes together by building support and contributing to the political process. In still another variation, public managers and policy analysts are seen as a responsible guild, drawing on their competence and professional training to implement higher ideas and meet needs. The core element of these variations is the technical expertise and competence of the public professional in contributing to and influencing the policy process.

This view of governance and this determination of the public interest—by professionalism and expertise—both complements and confronts Plenary Review. It complements Plenary Review in that expertise and knowledge can inform policy discussions and feed into legislative and executive considerations. It confronts the Plenary Review assumption that the constitutional branches can (and should) make policy decisions which guide the polity. Plenary Review is traditional in assigning this role primarily to the legislature and the executive, rather than choosing to place this responsibility in the hands of technical expertise and professional administration.

Political Realists

A last group of assumptions about how and where the public interest is determined is the "realist" view of the pluralistic group process. The pluralist group interplay, as discussed in earlier sections, is assumed to result in what is, in fact, the public interest. The outcome of this process is legitimized as the best collective choice because it has gathered support from disparate individuals and groups; it has also gone through the refining fire of debate, bargaining, attack and defense. Some see this pluralistic interplay almost as a mechanical process. Others see the process as providing insight and understanding of the public will and the benefits and liabilities to any particular action. Others rely on a "due process" interpretation assuming that a process which is fair and responsive will serve to ascertain the public interest. If care is taken to insure due process, it is maintained, then the outcome can be accepted as the public interest.

Plenary Review is not incompatible with these assumptions about the pushes and pulls of the pluralistic political process. Since Plenary Review does not aim to change political motivations or political actions, it does not directly confront these assumptions. A Plenary Review process would simply work more effectively within the influence of the pluralistic process. Plenary Review would accommodate the political pluralistic system, retaining the actions of the traditional branches as the legitimate governance mechanism while enhancing the effectiveness of both of them.

Assumptions about the Public Interest

Of course, most people do not state their arguments in the terms and framework which have just been used. But these assumptions undergird most preferences on how to improve the governance system and which entities should provide leadership. Is the President the responsible agent to take the lead in current times? The Congress? The Supreme Court? Or will technical processes, expertise and policy analysis guide and help the system? Or is salvation in the politics of the pluralistic process?

People rely on different bodies and processes to determine the public interest and people have different assumptions about governance. These preferences and assumptions greatly influence any evaluation of Plenary Review. Discussions about Plenary Review can end in impasse, because persons argue from different (and unrecognized) assumptions. For example, some may have serious objections to Plenary Review as unrealistic in the political process (political realists). Others argue that reliance on the legislature is foolhardy in these times; this is the century of the executive. Many academicians and policy professionals are anxious to show why policy analysis and various techniques should receive greater attention. Although no single indisputable evaluation of Plenary Review as governance action can convince everyone, there are two comments. First, the democratic variety of assumptions and approaches will benefit debate about Plenary Review and its contributions to governance. Second, none of these assumptions is incorrect because each describes parts and processes of the political system. As with the blind man and the elephant, all the seemingly disparate assumptions are part of an effective whole. Because one does not preclude the others, Plenary Review may strengthen the traditional system, while drawing from technical expertise and utilizing the pluralistic political process.

Some may argue that Plenary Review is not feasible, irrespective of whether it is a good idea or not. The appropriate strategy for such a situation, however, is to prepare, develop and try a good idea, even if it is not immediately practical. Victor Hugo pointed out that nothing is so powerful as an idea whose time has come. Dror noted that "feasibility changes with time, and some ideas need an extended period to ripen and gain acceptance" (1986: 269). Plenary Review will likely have to be practiced in minor applications before the architecture of public policy processes is significantly altered. Difficult as it may be, Plenary Review is well worth the experiment.

GOVERNANCE WORTHY OF DEMOCRATIC IDEALS

Plenary Review has been presented as evaluation of macro-policy and determination of future general direction. For public policy bodies in their governance responsibilities, Plenary Review enables statesmanship, stewardship and continuous watchfulness. These three terms capture that grand level of responsible governance to which democracies aspire. With respect to the first, the 1946 Congressional Reorganization Act contains a wonderful phrase. It assigns the standing committees of Congress the responsibility of maintaining "continuous watchfulness" in their areas of jurisdiction and assignment (see Scher, 1963: 526-528). For a policy body, Plenary Review provides a means to rise to this responsibility as watchman for the polity in continually assessing and guiding.

Second, Plenary Review can elevate policy bodies to a higher degree of statesmanship in governance decisions and actions. In his *Discourse on Statesmanship*, Paul Eidelberg described statesmanship as "the coordination of political theory and political practice" (1974: 3). This nicely describes the intent of Plenary Review. Decisions in guiding the polity are improved by carefully evaluating practice and regularly considering guiding principles and philosophies. Often enmeshed in the details of policy and program enactments, it is difficult for those involved in the development of public policy to rise to the level of statesmanship. Plenary Review is a perspective and approach which regularly encourages and enables a higher response.

Third, stewardship connotes serving established duties as well as overall governance responsibility for states of affairs and results. In a democratic system particularly, the established institutions and elected officials have an inescapable stewardship responsibility. In a final accounting, stewards may have given honest effort but can be found to be lacking in judgement and responsibility, especially if results have gone in an undesired—even if unintended—direction. It is important to anticipate where the system is going, what the particulars add up to, what the past and prospective consequences have been and may be, and what directive action should be taken. Plenary Review is intended to strengthen exactly this capacity.

Plenary Review is a way to escape the trap of thinking in the narrow terms so often necessary in particular programs or policies. Asking important questions, assessing consequences, and deliberating appropriate directions will develop insights and creative options. The perspective and the focus in Plenary Review will lead to thinking which will be beneficial to the democratic system. Vision should ensue from deliberation on values and goals. Periodic review and action incorporate self-reshaping abilities. Experience and feed-back instill learning by doing. New ways of thinking in Plenary Review have the potential of significant contributions to the polity and its policy making culture.

Pascal's famous wager is applicable here. Pascal argued that a wise man, not knowing if there were a God or an afterlife, should wager for the life of belief since there is almost nothing to lose and much to gain. An attempt—either as a general system or through selected efforts—to assess the moral, economic, social, political and institutional consequences, to deliberate guiding purposes, to take appropriate action, and to periodically repeat has almost nothing to lose but much to gain. Although some may take a deterministic view that what will be can not be avoided, improvements in the public policy system are clearly needed and should be made. Plenary Review will enable our polity to rise to its governance challenges and respond with the best of which we are capable.

FIVE: EVALUATING THE PLENARY REVIEW CONCEPT

There are two summary questions about the Plenary Review concept and public policy which are critical to discuss. First, can Plenary Review provide high quality policy making? Second, will the partial redesign of the policy process in adding Plenary Review be beneficial? This chapter will measure Plenary Review against these questions.

While neither Plenary Review nor any other decision format can *ensure* the perfect or optimum decision, it is possible to note the influence of Plenary Review on decisions and the decision process. The reader will recall two points presented in Chapter Three. First, the elements of Plenary Review exert a transforming and beneficial influence on policy decisions. Second, Plenary Review does not argue that the "right," or even the very "best," decision is always achieved. Plenary Review simply attempts to attain the "best available" decision which can be made through always limited information and the foresight of decision makers at a particular time. It assumes that attempting to evaluate the policy consequences, discern future needs and establish general guiding purposes will be much better than not attempting to do so. And Plenary Review does not require that the decision be perfect in each iteration. Periodic assessment is central to the Plenary Review concept, and each decision will again be reviewed in a few years and adjustments made with the best attainable decision at that time. Considering these points, there are some evaluative judgements which can be made about the Plenary Review approach and its policy decisions.

PLENARY REVIEW AND HIGH QUALITY POLICY MAKING

There is no one simple list of criteria to evaluate policy decisions acceptable to all public policy practitioners and scholars. However, a number of factors can be noted which generally contribute to high quality policy making. Table 5-1 lists some requisites of high quality policy making as a general basis for evaluating Plenary Review. The list is not presented as a formal or comprehensive model, nor as explicitly derived from empirical research. While the list is prescriptive and declarative, the individual factors would be highly compatible with much conventional wisdom about the policy process. The list draws from Nagel (1988: 15-57), Dror (1986: 139-217), Kingdon (1984) and Goggin (1990), as well as other sources. Following Table 5-1, Plenary Review will be compared to each of the points listed.

A policy system caught in the details and unable to discern those problems and issues which should have priority attention will be ineffective. Plenary Review will help governance bodies focus on important issues, problems and policies as it adds a periodic review of policy arenas to the natural percolation of issues. This governance level agenda setting—the recognition and prioritization of public policy issues and problems—is critical for an effective policy process.

Effective public policy must integrate a consideration of public goals with a disposition toward action. Doing should be linked with learning. Plenary Review directly incorporates value issues into the policy process and encourages action as best determined by general goals. Past policy consequences are evaluated to form macro-policy; macro-policy is then the basis for future action. The successive iteration of Plenary Review provides a mechanism to assess past consequences, feed them back, and adjust future actions. This is critical to responsiveness and adaptive policy learning.

TABLE 5-1
REQUISITES OF HIGH QUALITY POLICY MAKING

Policy systems will generally perform better as they:

- Focus on important issues and problems (agenda-setting)
- Integrate actions and goals
- Reconsider past policy actions and their consequences
- Enable feedback and policy adjustment
- Encourage different and insightful perspectives
- Provide a diagnostic framework
- Provide broad and long-term perspectives
- Encourage innovation and consideration of alternatives
- Establish a framework to handle complexity and uncertainty
- Avert crisis decision making
- Encourage policy leadership and governance actions
- Guide implementation and follow-up in regular evaluation
- Utilize pluralism and diversity in policy review
- Establish internal and external consistency
- Assess effectiveness--whether policies achieve as intended
- Consider equity including the assignment of benefits and costs

Policy orthodoxies should be reexamined regularly because present patterns can aggravate rigidity and stultify thinking. Such reconsideration provides for appropriate changes in direction or priorities. Plenary Review encourages new perspectives and a new way of responsible collective thinking in order to deal more effectively with the ever-changing challenges facing governance. Plenary Review adds an additional perspective to the current policy process. Insights will be added and understanding will be broadened as the Plenary Review format leads to deliberations on macro-policy, consequences and policy arenas.

An enhanced capacity for diagnosis is important to meet current deficiencies in policy making. In Plenary Review, the analysis of current situations benefits from a diagnostic framework which assesses past and prospective consequences of public policy and its implementation and deliberates guiding principles for future policy actions. The Plenary Review framework focuses attention on interrelated policies (in the policy arena) and encourages generalizations from the particulars in the establishment of macro-policy. An effective policy system must also include systematic consideration of broad and long-term perspectives. While Plenary Review itself may have many of the limitations built into any decision making system of individuals and institutions, it does encourage and require a broad and long-term focus, which is based in performance and outcomes.

Under some conditions, incrementalism is an adequate mode for policy making. Other challenges and contexts call for more change and innovation. To the current incremental system, Plenary Review adds the capacity to assess current outcomes, broaden choices and determine desired future developments. This will support innovation and change. At the minimum, Plenary Review adds alternate views and concerns to open policy debate. At the maximum, Plenary Review could be a form of public policy entrepreneurship as it establishes different perspectives, enhances the capacities of those selected to govern, leads to policy strategies and institutes a regular means for creative adjustments. As in entrepreneurial effort, insight is linked with leadership.

A high quality policy approach must handle complexity well. Plenary Review provides a framework of values and outcome assessments within which complexities can be thoughtfully and deliberately investigated. An effective policy system must be able to choose among ill-defined possibilities and uncertainties, with the aim of affecting the probability of alternative futures. In most important public policy contexts, outcomes are uncertain and probabilities are only statistical estimates; both non-decision and incremental decisions can be quite inadequate and change occurs frequently. There must be some sophistication about different kinds and degrees of uncertainty, and about taking calculated risks. While Plenary Review does not automatically build in such risk-taking calculation and sophistication, it does encourage both of them through open assessment of consequences, debate over desirable ends, while the policy process is seen as developmental and adaptive. The broader scope in Plenary Review is able to rise to the level in which such complexity can be better handled.

A public policy system which is not able either to anticipate crises or react in their early stages will find options more limited at the very time the challenge is increasing rapidly. Plenary Review helps to avert crisis decision making by regularly reviewing major policy arenas and assessing consequences. This can be expected to expand policy alternatives and to reduce policy problems. But were a crisis to develop, how would Plenary Review work in such a situation? Crisis reaction is not the intent or strength of Plenary Review, but it is still possible to develop a guiding macro-policy to meet a crisis through use of the Plenary Review perspective. In general, however, Plenary Review is intended rather to avert crisis reactions by periodically dealing with public policy arenas before the problems have mounted to the crisis stage. This is governance by deliberative anticipation of future needs, directions and priorities.

Leadership can strengthen the public policy process. More can be done simply by additional effort; it is seldom that the policy system utilizes fully its current capacities. Plenary Review provides a mechanism for more effective policy leadership as well as increasing the deliberative effort directed toward public policy. Plenary Review will focus on the more significant guiding policies, rather than being tied closely to policy detail. Plenary Review assists those in governance capacities to have a clearer focus, to assess past and prospective consequences and to deliberate on the most appropriate current ends and actions, in the reasonable expectation that decisions will be more effective and productive.

Plenary Review guides future implementation and then regularly checks the results of that implementation. Policy design, even when adequate, can flounder in the details of operation and implementation. Plenary Review contributes to implementation in two ways. First, it provides a guiding direction to be followed in interpretations and applications. Second, it provides a periodic review of the outcomes of implementation, followed by appropriate adjustments. And even further, the policy as actually carried out is considered, not just the formal statement of that policy. Plenary Review will be particularly needed in cases where there are developing needs for major changes in policy but the administrative structure is not yet fully responsive.

Pluralistic deliberation is an essential element of an effective policy system in a democracy. Plenary Review attempts to develop enlightenment for both lay and elite participants in the broader and longer term aspects of public policy. Plenary Review encourages diversity, advocacy, debate and discussion ending with a decision. It is designed to work within the pluralism of democracy, not supplant it, as indeed many planning mechanisms tend to do.

High quality policy making must establish both internal and external consistency. Effective policy must be consistent within its own provisions and with its own guiding philosophy and intent. Policy should also be consistent with related policies and programs. Current policy processes in most policy bodies are not designed to insure such consistency, although it does periodically occur, frequently through extraordinary effort. Plenary Review provides a framework to integrate policies both internally and externally.

Nagel listed effectiveness as one of the three main criteria to evaluate public policies (Nagel, 1988: 29-57). To be effective, policy systems must include some device to insure that policies achieve that which they are intended to achieve. As opposed to the current policy process, Plenary Review is designed to regularly review the intended and unintended consequences in policy arenas. Without such regular feedback, adjustment is not possible and policies are less guided toward intended purposes.

An important governance responsibility is the choice between the "unchooseable," the necessity "to allocate order of priority and relative weights to values and goals, all of which are absolute in themselves" (Dror, 1986: 190). The need to make a decision, with costs imposed on particular groups and benefits given to various groups, is a difficult challenge. This is the concern of equity, a central criterion for the effectiveness of public policy (Nagel, 1988: 29-57). The choices in spreading benefits and costs and determining their maximum and minimum levels are not easily made. It is ordinarily very difficult for democracies and representative assemblies to make such critical judgements, and they are often avoided when possible. Plenary Review assists in handling such difficulties by recognizing consequences, selecting desirable ends and debating actions in a systematic and deliberative way. Nagel concluded that the criteria of effectiveness, efficiency and equity, endorse "a more favorable attitude toward generality, societal improvement, clarity of definitions, clarity of goals, concern for relations and simplicity" (Nagel, 1988: 56). These, of course, are

Evaluating the Concept

the focus of Plenary Review. The clarification of macro-policy should lead to the "best possible" evaluations for the future directions in public policy.

Plenary Review is not, of course, presented as a panacea for all policy problems in our governance system. However, in its concept and intent Plenary Review has the potential to make a significant contribution to more effective public policy. It provides both a new perspective and a mechanism to increase and strengthen the efforts of those with public policy responsibilities. Plenary Review would contribute steadily to the adaptation and effectiveness of the system.

TABLE 5-2
PLENARY REVIEW AND
HIGH QUALITY POLICY MAKING

Plenary Review generally results in high quality policy making because it:

- Identifies important issues and problems

- Integrates goals and actions in policy making

- Encourages thinking in ways which go beyond current policy approaches and stimulates alternatives

- Expands efforts to analyze and understand policy problems based on the consequences of past policy

- Reviews policy periodically to identify issues, assess changing needs and take action

- Adapts through repeated cycles of assessment and action

- Directs attention from details to general policy purposes and principles and provides a diagnostic framework

- Concentrates deliberative effort on the improvement of public policies

- Intervenes before the crisis stage

- Enables policy makers to act more effectively

- Encourages a pluralistic and deliberative process

- Directs attention to concerns of equity

REDESIGN OF THE POLICY PROCESS

The previous section measured Plenary Review against the requisites of high quality policy. This section will evaluate Plenary Review as a redesign of the public policy system. Dror developed both principles (substantive ideas to serve as guides for redesign) and strategies (ways to make redesigns more feasible) (1986: 254-272). These principles and strategies—listed in Table 5-3—will be used to assess Plenary Review.

TABLE 5–3
PRINCIPLES AND STRATEGIES FOR POLICY MAKING REDESIGN

Redesign of policy making systems should include:
• Taboos Must Be Broken
• Limits of the Material Should Be Carefully Considered
• Political Feasibility Requires Aggressive Handling
• Build Extensively, But Not Exclusively, on Available Experiences
• Redesign Should Focus on Most Urgent Needs
• Avoid Simple Schemata and Models
• Avoid Dogmas and Slogans
• Institutionalize Effort Allocation
• Assurance of Integrative Perspective
• Positive Redundancy Is a Useful Construction Principle
• Introduce Additional Types of Knowledge
• Prepare Good Redesign Ideas, Even If Not Immediately Practical
• Build Up a Capacity for Policy Making Redesign

Source: Dror, 1986: 254-272; nine items not listed.

There is little chance for significant improvement in redesign of the policy process unless attempts are made to go beyond the current process, or in Dror's terms, taboos are broken. New approaches and processes must be considered. Plenary Review is one attempt to go beyond the current processes to establish new approaches.

The limits of the elements in the policy system—such as human limitations, the dynamic interaction of groups and incomplete information—must be respected. The policy process can not be redesigned while ignoring human behavior and the dynamics of human institutions. Plenary Review is designed to operate within current human and institutional considerations.

Dror commented that the political feasibility of policy redesigns may be greater than most of the literature assumes. He has suggested an aggressive approach, building extensively, but not exclusively, on available experiences (1986: 257-258). Such is also the philosophy in the Plenary Review effort. Plenary Review adds a complementary mode which builds on the current public policy system. As Plenary Review elements compensate for some important deficiencies in the current system, it strengthens that system. And Plenary Review has been developed through discussions, experiments, simulations and projects (reported in Chapter Seven) which deal with real issues in the real world. Redesign efforts should be built on the urgent needs not well met in the current public policy process. Plenary Review carefully assesses major policy arenas and takes the broad perspective to discern critical needs and issues. It selects those areas requiring attention at the important level of macro-policy.

Any effort to redesign the policy process must balance realism with innovative abstractions and generalizations. It is difficult to avoid simplistic schemes and models—and some might so label the Plenary Review concept. Although Plenary Review incorporates a large measure of idealism, it attempts to ground its recommendations in the realities of the political system. Plenary Review does attempt to develop guiding directions; it attempts to model through, not muddle through. Simple dogmas and slogans have been eschewed for confidence in deliberations which systematically consider and act on the important factors from the most helpful perspectives.

Dror has contended there is a need to relieve—to use his term—the central minds of governments of unessential matters by delegating most detailed matters to executive and administrative functions, while establishing a special track for critical issues. Effort should be allocated to major rather than minor issues and this should be institutionalized in the policy redesign. Plenary Review matches these points well in both intent and design.

The criteria of an integrative perspective and redundancy are also met in Plenary Review. By its nature, Plenary Review integrates through selecting arenas of policies for regular attention and through recognizing past and prospective consequences. Redundancy is found in the requirement to take a second and more general look at policy, particularly in its past and prospective outcomes. In Plenary Review, the regular legislative or policy body enactment is not of itself sufficient for good public policy outcomes; a regular review to check implementation, reevaluate intent and redirect goals improves the processes of public policies. Beneficial redundancy in the Plenary Review concept will also occur through overlapping arenas and their interactive consequences.

Plenary Review introduces additional types of knowledge through encouraging the kind of thinking required to meet the challenges. Plenary Review encourages such new thinking in four ways. First, it provides policy making with added philosophic underpinning. The broad view, focus on moral and social consequences and establishment of general guiding directions necessarily engage the philosophic questions which underpin policy. Second, historic, societal and comparative perspectives arise from the periodic assessments. Third, actual practice is integrated with goals, particularly in the evaluation of consequences. Fourth, Plenary Review enlarges the area of deliberation both horizontally in considering related policies and vertically in moving to a higher level of generality in macro-policy.

Dror's last two criteria are preparing redesign ideas and building capacity. Plenary Review is an example of each. Plenary Review proposes a good redesign idea, even if not immediately practical. The effort is guided by what might—and should—be. Focusing merely on what is currently feasible is shortsighted. Plenary Review will build up the capacity for change and improvement of the policy system, especially as it provides regular review and adjustment.

In summary, Plenary Review meets many of the strategies and principles for redesign of the policy process. Plenary Review has the potential to be a significant redesign of the policy system.

Most individuals desire improvements in the policy making system. However, some may argue that improvements should be made within the current system (make it work more effectively) rather than

Evaluating the Concept

change the system itself (through some reconceptualization or redesign). Plenary Review does not, of course, negate attempts to make improvements within the current system. The public policy system can still be improved through more effective development of the current structure and process. In Congress, for example, improvements might be made in legislative organization and procedures. However, such improvements will not be equal to all the challenges. The challenges and needs require something more such as the complementary Plenary Review mode. This mode can make a great contribution in new ways of thought and action not possible in the current system.

TABLE 5-4
PLENARY REVIEW AND
CHANGE IN THE POLICY SYSTEM

Plenary Review matches many principles and strategies for redesign of the public policy process because it:

- Breaks out of current limitations through a new approach
- Recognizes and works within political, human and institutional constraints
- Takes an aggressive stance toward political feasibility
- Builds extensively, but not exclusively, on available experiences and information
- Focuses on macro-policy rather than becoming enmeshed in policy and program details
- Integrates through use of policy arenas
- Incorporates adaptive learning and "debugging" through periodic reviews and adjustments
- Introduces additional perspectives and information into the policy process
- Thinks in levels of magnitude appropriate to current policy challenges
- Prepares useful ideas and alternatives even if not immediately practical

Plenary Review
and Public Policy

Public policy is the aggregate of consequences flowing from actions taken by public bodies. Plenary Review is intended to be a separate and distinct mode of deliberation by a public policy body. Plenary Review is a regular, periodic review of such consequences (social, moral, economic, political and institutional) in a specified arena of public policy by a policy body. The product of Plenary Review is a statement of guiding direction for that specified arena. The statement of guiding direction will describe the desired future consequences to be achieved and will be used to guide future actions. This statement is to be fully acknowledged in each subsequent specific action within that arena. Each acknowledgement is to contain either an explicit confirmation of the statement or a clear justification of departures.

This chapter has compared Plenary Review to the requisites of high quality policy making and the principles and strategies for policy making redesign. Plenary Review measures well against these standards. Plenary Review can make a significant contribution to the public policy system.

PART II:
APPLICATIONS OF PLENARY REVIEW

The first five chapters have presented the Plenary Review concept. The general description of Plenary Review has raised important questions of operation and application. The following chapters now move from the concept to its use. Chapter Six will focus on possible operational details. Chapter Seven will review the development of Plenary Review and its experimental applications to this point. Chapter Eight will apply Plenary Review to a wide variety of settings. Chapter Nine will discuss possible uses of Plenary Review in the U.S. Congress. Chapter Ten will conclude with a discussion of the challenges of adopting Plenary Review in public policy bodies.

As the focus shifts from the basic concept to its application, the presentation necessarily becomes more speculative and conjectural. Since Plenary Review has been applied in only limited uses, much developmental work remains to be done. The following chapters make suggestions and report experiments with the operational applications of Plenary Review at the same time that it is recognized that the application of any new concept will require further development based on experience and use. The Interactivity Foundation and the author invite questions, suggestions and projects which might better help to develop Plenary Reviews operations and applications.

SIX: THE CONDUCT AND OPERATION OF PLENARY REVIEW

The general description of Plenary Review in Part I did not delve extensively into all the important questions about its conduct and operation. This chapter responds to such practical questions: How might it work? Who has the authority to authorize and initiate Plenary Review? How are policy arenas determined? How can policy arenas be scheduled for periodic review? What format is required for discussion and deliberation in Plenary Review? How is the knowledge and insight from policy implementers incorporated in Plenary Review? How are Plenary Review decisions made? What is a guiding direction and what does it do? How is the guiding direction implemented? These and related concerns will be reviewed in this Chapter.

One caveat should be made explicit at this point. There are many different methods to conduct Plenary Review and there are many degrees to which it can be implemented. This Chapter presents some illustrations and suggestions without assuming that these combine in the only approach. Various permutations are possible in different applications. It is also important to note that this presentation on the operation of Plenary Review illustrates that Plenary Review is conceptually possible and that it can potentially contribute to the effectiveness of a variety of policy bodies, especially the U.S. Congress.

INITIATION OF PLENARY REVIEW

Who has the authority to establish a Plenary Review system and the authority to initiate and authorize the Plenary Review of a policy arena? In most policy bodies, the authority to establish a Plenary Review system and to perform a specific Plenary Review is inherent. That is, a city council or the national Congress has inherent power to have a Plenary Review discussion and to establish guiding directions. They also have the power to establish a process whereby policy arenas are reviewed periodically and macro-policy established. A comprehensive Plenary Review system would have to be adopted by the total body, of course, but individual committees could establish Plenary Review processes and perspectives within their own jurisdictions. Small bodies can periodically move into a separate Plenary Review mode. Large bodies may want to charge various committees and subcommittees to perform a Plenary Review on specific policy arenas and report them to the body at large for review and adoption.

Although it adds a second mode, Plenary Review is specifically intended to fit most public policy bodies. Most bodies largely control their own format and deliberative process and can internally establish a Plenary Review system by action of the body. In the Congress, for example, a Plenary Review system could be created by congressional rule. (It might also be mandated by constitutional amendment or established by statutory action.) In fact, Plenary Review can also be accomplished informally without any authorizing action by, say, one committee deliberating macro-policy and informally accepting guidelines for their actions in a particular policy arena, or one subcommittee on retreat taking a Plenary Review perspective for the policy arenas in their jurisdiction. As experience develops, these more informal applications will likely precede and provide the base for the adoption of more comprehensive Plenary Review processes.

Although Plenary Review can be operated informally, it is important to develop a Plenary Review process to identify policy arenas, schedule periodic review, provide a separate mode of deliberation and create a permanent cycle. A critical reason for a formal and authorized process is that it empowers the result by giving the guiding direction standing and enabling appropriate follow-up actions to be taken. This process distinguishes Plenary Review from the policy analysis of various committees, policy institutes and think-tanks.

Plenary Review as Agenda Setting

In its full application, Plenary Review enables the policy body in due course to review each major policy arena. The policy body thus creates an agenda for review which would cover all major policy arenas in their responsibility, whether this be a legislature or a subcommittee. However, some flexibility should allow additional Plenary Reviews for new policy arenas of current significance. New policy arenas will arise in the policy agenda from participant and citizen concern, recognition of important problems and significant events (see Kingdon, 1984: 16 19, 206 209; Asher & Weisberg, 1985: 423).

The Plenary Review agenda is crucial because it leads directly to an agenda of government, to the formulation and modification of governance policies, and to the subsequent programs and policies which flow from the macro-policy. Since the setting of the agenda is the initiating stage of policy making and implementing actions (Ripley, 1987: 2), it is important to review policy arenas and identify those items requiring more immediate action. The Plenary Review process is an important agenda setting device because it can be used to review, in some suitable sequence, major policy arenas and raise important items to debate and decision. As a general process, Plenary Review can be seen as essentially a "policy scan," which begins with an old or undetermined policy agenda and ends with a revised or confirmed one. The evaluative and broad view, characteristic of Plenary Review, will bring to the surface many complex policy matters which require attention, review and future guidance.

Institutionalizing Plenary Review

Plenary Review is best established in a formally adopted, separate mode and schedule. After formal adoption, of course, there will be challenges to effective operation. Practical experience and research findings alike confirm that decision approaches are frequently more difficult to operate than anticipated. This is well illustrated by various techniques to improve policy and budget decisions. Techniques such as ZBB (zero-base budgeting), sunset legislation, strategic planning and PPBS (planning-programming-budgeting systems) have had difficulty in matching hopes (see Lauth, 1985; Schick and Hatry, 1982; and Swiss, 1991).

The factors which will help a Plenary Review system to become and to remain effective are a serious challenge which will benefit from additional thought, development, research and experimentation. This chapter will present many ideas which will contribute toward an effective system and the chapter on adoption will make suggestions as well. The chapter on Plenary Review in the U.S. Congress will compare Plenary Review to sunset legislation, oversight, budget and planning efforts. However, these all fall short of insuring an effective Plenary Review system. Further research on ZBB, PPBS, strategic planning and such may yield insights into operational problems and approaches, which might be useful in Plenary Review; however, this goes beyond the current presentation.

The frank recognition of these operational problems does not warrant inaction or dismissal of the Plenary Review concept. The revisions in the congressional budget system do not work perfectly, but there is more coordination, better schedules and more guidance than without the revisions. Indeed, a Plenary Review system might work well—it should not be assumed that it won't. Experience with Plenary Review and recognition of its benefits might contribute to a growing effectiveness. Even so, we will need to act with imperfect and incomplete systems. This is a case where "the perfect is an enemy of the good" if we wait for the perfect system. As Swiss noted, if public officials wait until they can institute a system that is comprehensive and fully effective in operation, they will wait forever (Swiss, 1991: x). Recognizing these limitations, the Chapter now proceeds to consider how such a system might work.

Definition of the Policy Arena

How is the appropriate scope of policy review determined? Too narrow a focus will miss other very relevant policies, problems and programs which overlap and will limit insight. Too broad a focus ineffectively relates to too much. Each new integration of policies or programs advances complexity by geometrical progression (Sundquist, 1981: 437-438).

The unit of analysis in Plenary Review is the "policy arena." Programs related to one another are joined to constitute a policy arena. For example, a specific program is the Urban Development Action Grant (UDAG), but the policy arena would be urban development. Such broadening of levels is critical to the development of useful policy alternatives and governance decisions. A Plenary Review of federal urban economic development policies and programs should be able to compare different philosophies and delivery systems rather than evaluate only one program, one set of assumptions or one approach. An important trade-off to be considered in drawing an arena boundary is the trade-off between depth and scope. Some depth often will have to be sacrificed to comprehend better the interrelationship of several related programs; the focus must include both the program specifics (critical in evaluation) and the general context in which a program operates.

While the aggregation of programs and policies created for review is important, there can be no simple drawing of boundaries, because the linkages which could be considered never end. Multiple and overlapping boundaries are appropriate since different programs contribute to multiple arenas and might properly be included in their review. For example, tobacco policy might be part of macro-policies in both agriculture and health and clean air might be considered in both environmental and economic development guiding directions. Since some arenas will have considerable flux, policy arenas can be flexible and changeable. For example, rapid changes in technological issues would require redefinition and reformulation of macro-policies influenced by these changes. The logic of selecting and delimiting policy arenas rests in the network of relations that describe and give insight to patterns of causality and consequences. The policy body should use judgement in delineating and modifying policy arenas.

The policy arena for Plenary Review certainly should not be seen as an isolated or narrowly defined program. Arenas must be carefully described to recognize the continuing interactivity, interrelationship and interdependence of policies and programs. The choice of perspective will very much depend on the nature of the policy problem with which the policy body is dealing (Morgan, 1986: 252). The definition of the policy arena should be made by the body conducting the Plenary Review as one of the initial concerns. Since many policies and programs unavoidably interact, this relationship should be understood while making choices which delimit and circumscribe. Recognition of interaction can broaden and deepen analysis, and by not avoiding complexity, may even suggest new approaches and new solutions. While it may not always be possible to neatly describe the focal area, the concept of policy arena—of interacting policies and programs over several areas—is necessary to effective perspectives and improved insights. This is the step up to macro-policy from specific policies and programs.

In most cases, the focus should be a problem issue area or macro-policy, to which various policies and programs are directed. For example, rather than focus on a program such as food stamps, a problem or issue focus would consider welfare and poverty matters. The policy arena should be drawn beyond existing programs and policies so that it is not limited to past actions, but can anticipate issues and identify unmet needs. Although general policy arenas will be determined and scheduled, Plenary Review arenas are essentially what the Plenary Review body says they are.

Periodic Review

In a comprehensive system of Plenary Review, periodic review cycles are established to cover all major policy arenas. The public policy body generally has the authority to establish its own review cycle. In larger policy bodies where there are specialized subunits, the body as a whole establishes the review cycles and charges the committees and subcommittees.

Sunset legislation systems generally use a seven-year cycle. In such a system, review of agencies and programs is scheduled to distribute the yearly workload. A similar system could also work well for Plenary Review; all major policy arenas might be reviewed over, say, a seven-year or ten-year cycle. Such a comprehensive review schedule ensures coverage of all major arenas and requires the periodic evaluation of difficult or overlooked topics.

A general review schedule can still allow some flexibility of choice and selection. All arenas may not require the same schedule of attention. Some arenas might change rapidly; others might be relatively stable. Surging or unforeseen events could indicate an immediate need in some arenas for a review of consequences and the establishment of guiding directives more often than every seven or ten years. Other policy arenas may not yet be quite ripe for review as scheduled; there may be stages in some policy arenas when initial review might suggest postponement. It is, however, important to have some clear regular system for periodic reviews, while permitting some adjustment in the rigid schedule.

Comprehensive Listing of Policies

As the policy body describes policy arenas, they should group them into a comprehensive listing of public policies. As developed, the listing of policies can be used to schedule review. Although Plenary

Review may develop its own comprehensive listing of public policies for review, it could utilize or draw from existing classification systems. At the federal level, for example, there are a number of current policy classification systems. The United States Code organizes enactments into various titles and topics. The Program Planning Budgeting System (PPBS) developed in the sixties and the Zero-Base Budget system (ZBB) in the seventies both organized topical program areas for review. The congressional committee and subcommittee structure is in itself a classification system. The congressional functional arrangement would be easier to adopt than other classification systems, would require less congressional change and would strengthen the congressional units to develop coordinated programs in their several areas of responsibility (see Davidson & Oleszek, 1977: 59). The Subcommittee on the Legislative Process (of the House Rules Committee) created an inventory of programs (arranged by committee jurisdiction) as part of their efforts to improve sunset review and oversight (US House, Rules, 1980: 118). In short, a Plenary Review listing of public policies will need to be developed to organize policy arenas, schedule their review and make assignments where subunits are involved.

Timely Decisions

Timely action is important for effective Plenary Review. For example, Congress would be ineffective in either the regular legislative mode or the Plenary Review mode if it ignores its responsibilities or just does not get around to them in the press of other items. Plenary Review will benefit from a mechanism that requires review. Three provisions help to meet this need. First, a cycle for Plenary Review should be established so that policy arenas are reviewed on a regular basis. Second, a distinct and designated Plenary Review mode and time should be established in the policy body. Third, Plenary Review should be adopted with the requirement to perform regular reviews.

These provisions are important to provide Plenary Review with a responsible action focus. There are many excellent policy analyses emanating from scholars, policy institutes and a wide variety of other sources, but they are impotent without an authoritative decision and without action by the responsible body. The key is an action focus in a responsible body. Unless policy review is empowered and responsible—that is, plenary—review is often disappointing and leads nowhere. Plenary Review attempts to build in both the deliberative and action elements needed in public policy. Although there can be excellent policy analysis outside Congress or other policy bodies, a major need is to tie policy review to an action and enabling focus. The two parts of the policy process must be effectively joined.

Should a complementary Plenary Review process be added to Congress when the operational pressures and current demands are already unrelenting? Current constraints seem to preclude most activities and functions beyond that already on the agenda (Oppenheimer, 1985: 396). However, this is also a problem which a Plenary Review mode might help solve. A Plenary Review mode in the Congress or other policy body requiring periodic review and scheduling time for deliberation of macro-policy may contribute to the effectiveness and efficiency of the regular policy mode. (A later chapter will consider possible changes in Congress which might also deal with the crucial problem of time constraints.)

DELIBERATIVE FORMAT

Plenary Review does not require any single structured format for its deliberations and decisions. Plenary Review is purposely intended to be usable in a variety of formats, particularly the existing processes of most policy and legislative bodies. However, there are some factors which facilitate Plenary Review; these will be discussed in this section.

The core elements of Plenary Review are best accomplished in an open and deliberative process. The particular focus and the intended judgements in Plenary Review are generally not realized well in a closely limited, controlled or hierarchical setting. Policy decisions involving complex and longer term issues are likely to be more satisfactorily deliberated in the open, representative and democratic setting of most policy bodies (such as Congress), rather than by the more hierarchical processes of the executive or administrative bureaucracies. Consideration of ideas, pluralistic interplay, judgement and interest interaction can be most effective in a focused deliberative setting. Deliberation also has a refining and enlarging impact on the view of each participant in the policy body (Eidelberg, 1974: 156-157). Opinions are not just *ex*changed, but *changed* or modified through deliberation. Eidelberg has contended that "deliberation about alternative courses of action and about their immediate and long-term consequences is a learning process which places in question the adequacy or soundness of previously held opinions. Agreement

Conduct and Operation

on a common course of action involves commitment which may alter attitudes and expectations" (1974: 156-157). A deliberative and participative format enables the interaction necessary to perspectives and analysis.

A deliberative format does make a difference. Different decision formats are better adapted to different policy levels and types of policy discussions. Randall Ripley has contended that there are currently different decision-making patterns for different types of policy statements (1983: 392). He described the difference in decision patterns arising from such different types as distributive, competitive regulatory, protective regulatory, redistributive, structural, strategic and crisis policy. In a later work, Ripley illustrated how characteristics of the conduct of the actors, their relationships, the degree of visibility of the decision, and the influence of the President, bureaus, Congress, congressional subcommittees and the private sector will be different in different policy types (1987: 22-23). Forester reviewed different approaches to decision-making and concluded that different contexts call for correspondingly different strategies of action (1984: 22-31). Sagoff compared ethical and political judgements with cost-benefit analysis and welfare economics and then noted that the approach used and the questions asked determine a great deal what the outcome will be (1988: 39). The Plenary Review decision format must be deliberative and participative in order to fit the level of macro-policy, deal with value questions, assess consequences and determine public policy purposes. Since most policy and legislative bodies employ deliberative processes, Plenary Review does not require a large change from current practice.

The Information Base for Plenary Review

Deliberations and decisions are, of course, greatly influenced by the information which is being considered. Legislators—or others conducting Plenary Review—will bring their own knowledge and experience to Plenary Review discussions, but additional information will need to be considered in Plenary Review deliberations. Information is a key source for recognition of past consequences and for judgements on necessary actions. There are two internal sources of information which add greatly to Plenary Review. The first is a stewardship report prepared by implementing executives and administrators. The second source of information would be prepared by staff to the policy body or the body itself. In addition, information should be drawn from interested groups and experts outside the policy body.

The Stewardship Report

Knowledge and information from the implementing experience in that policy arena can add important insights to a policy body. Stewardship reports from the responsible executives and administrators should provide important current information for most Plenary Review deliberations. Stewardship reports will not be without a particular perspective, bias or policy view; indeed, the stewardship report should give not only the current descriptive information and explanation of performance, but the executive and administrative rationale and pertinent recommendations as well. By having the officials responsible for the administrative or executive performance report on the present policy design and its impact, policy bodies are exposed directly to the critical aspects of the public policy as it is being implemented. Such stewardship reports prepared specifically for each Plenary Review policy arena would be both valuable enterprises and products. The public policy body should request the responsible executives and administrators to submit stewardship reports for each policy arena to be reviewed.

The aspect of the stewardship report which is critical to Plenary Review is the rationale underpinning a public policy arena as it is actually being applied and implemented. The stewardship report need not be strictly objective or even clearly neutral. Indeed, it usually should reflect the point of view of the executive and responsible administrators, and these may or may not accord with the original policy body or legislative intent. Nevertheless, that perspective, even if sometimes too narrow, is essential for Plenary Review participants in the policy body to understand. At a minimum, agencies should report on the broad outlines of their operation and the costs of their policy implementation; they should compare objectives with accomplishments; they should recommend changes and discuss overall philosophy. Information on effectiveness and consequences should also be included. The information designed for the sunset review process is illustrative of the kind of information required for Plenary Review (see US, House, Rules Committee, 1980: 125-126, for required sunset data and program inventory information proposed in the Sunset Review Act of 1979).

Staff Support and Information

Additional information and reports should be provided by staff agencies to the policy body or developed by the policy body itself. In many cases, the policy body may want to use existing staff organizations to prepare the background information. For example, the Congress might utilize general staff agencies such as the General Accounting Office, Congressional Reference Service and Congressional Budget Office or staff connected to committees and subcommittees. Where desired, a special Plenary Review staff could be established to gather information for the Plenary Review process as well as perform specified preliminary studies. Such a staff could be similar to the legislative research arms which some states have established for their sunset legislation systems.

The support staff should both prepare and gather basic information on the policy arena for use by the policy body. They might conduct research projects as directed. They should gather extant reports and information relevant to the topic at hand. At the federal level, for example, they would collect annual reports, topical reviews (such as the *Economic Report of the President*), program evaluations, analytical studies and other similar efforts from the executive and legislative branches. Additional information from experts, policy institutes, administrators of related programs, academics, think-tanks and other interested individuals and associations might also be gathered in advance of the Plenary Review of a public policy arena.

The Plenary Review support staff may also be directed to track key indicators in important policy arenas. This might build on the efforts since the mid-1960s to construct social indicators or social policy statistics. In *Policy Indicators: Links Between Social Science and Public Debate*, Duncan MacRae, Jr., has reviewed the movement to add social indicators to existing economic and other indicators (1985). Such approaches, which attempt to measure trends and policy consequences, might also be directly useful in Plenary Review.

Various information banks and data bases may be useful to Plenary Review analysis and deliberations. These may include both existing data sources and information banks created for Plenary Review. This brief discussion of data bases and key indicators only illustrates possibilities which should be considered. There is yet much developmental work and thought which might creatively be applied to the information support for Plenary Review.

Information from External Sources

In addition to the stewardship report, staff studies and basic information, it is also important to understand the viewpoints of interested groups and experts. In these respects, Plenary Review will not differ greatly from current processes in Congress and other policy bodies. As desired, the policy body can receive testimony and information from various individuals and groups. This is a key responsibility of representation in a democracy, and policy bodies should consider such viewpoints in their Plenary Review deliberations.

Policy analyses emanating from a wide variety of external sources may also be useful in Plenary Review. These would include studies and recommendations from academic research centers, policy institutes, think-tanks, public forums and professional associations. These additional sources of information might enrich debate and provide alternative perspectives.

STATEMENT OF GUIDING DIRECTION

The end product of a Plenary Review of a policy arena is a guiding direction for that arena. A guiding direction evaluates past consequences and determines a vision of prospective public policy purposes. Regular policy statements and statutory legislation are contrasted with this general macro-policy as being far more specific in almost every case. Specific policies and programs are then enacted and implemented within the general guiding direction. As Plenary Review goes through subsequent cycles, the guiding statements will not be static but will themselves be reviewed in the periodic assessment of the policy arena and the developing sense of the macro-policy in each policy arena.

More specifically, a Plenary Review guiding direction includes: 1) an assessment of the moral, social, economic, political and institutional consequences of activities in the policy arena; 2) the specification of purposes which programs within the policy arena should achieve; 3) ends criteria for judgement in guiding future operations; 4) a discussion of anticipated future problems and needs which are to be met; 5) a sense of priorities for immediate policy actions in this arena; and 6) the delineation of various corrective actions if they have arisen in the deliberations.

At the federal level, Plenary Review guiding directions would form a framework for substantive policy purposes and macro-policy within the constitutional framework. The Plenary Review guiding direction compares to a more developed and honed "statement of purpose" section found at the beginning of most legislation. The guiding direction would describe selected end-values as a framework for legislative, regulatory and implementing actions within the policy system. Such a framework would operate as an ongoing guide to specific programs and their contributory actions. For illustration, a guiding statement on the environment might deal with human well-being, the quality of life and the interaction of biological systems and the physical world, rather than details on the specific concentration of polluting substances, forest management and so forth. A statement on income and poverty might discuss economic and material well-being, equity, needs, rights and minima for life; this would guide statutory concerns which deal with the details of various programs and regulations (adapted from MacRae, 1985: 38-39).

The guiding statement is intended to result in subsequent positive actions and adjustments, and not merely be findings and policy positions. The direction is intended to guide the policy arena into the future. Recognizing that there are no simple causes and that these matters are very complex, the Plenary Review guiding direction is intended to specify only general action and to frame interventions suitable to influence the pattern of development, but not specify all detailed actions, although they may be appended to the guiding direction as they result from deliberations by the policy body.

Corrective Action

The guidance of any policy arena can be done positively or it can be done negatively. A positive approach would establish guiding movements toward a desired state. A negative approach would detect error and institute corrective action to move toward the desired state. Plenary Review might utilize either or both approaches depending on the policy arena under consideration.

A core insight from cybernetics (the study of information, communication and control) is that "the ability of a system to engage in self-regulating behavior depends on processes of information exchange involving negative feedback. This process is central to the process of steersmanship" (Morgan, 1986: 84-87). In this concept, the accomplishment of many tasks is performed by corrective action rather than goal action. If a boat is off course by having the rudder too far in one direction, it gets back on course only by moving the rudder in the opposite direction. When an individual picks up an object, negative corrections center the hand so as better to grasp the object—through correction, we avoid failing to pick it up. The negative feedback and error correction of cybernetics may be a useful additional option as a means to control and steer policy.

The guiding direction in Plenary Review could indicate bounds for course correction and adjusting action. A constraint system, flexible but with real limits, could better accommodate some public policy arenas than positive action which depicts the objective and the steps to move toward it. A Plenary Review enactment might, in some instances, include negative constraints as well as positive statements. For example, the guiding direction might include constraints by unemployment levels which, if exceeded, would trigger various corrective actions. Or a guiding direction on environmental protection may specify guidelines for appropriate actions at various levels of pollution. The guiding direction might utilize a moving range in specifying actions for various contingencies.Plenary Review, both in positive and negative approaches, creates a *process* of review and action. It does not create a final list of end-results or principles which stand for all time, solve all normative questions and apply to all circumstances. In fact, it will almost always be necessary to take action and meet practical concerns without the possibility of knowing and understanding everything beforehand. The specification of either positive steps or negative constraints will be a part of the learning and developing decision process. Plenary Review creates a system where policy actions and their consequences are evaluated and general steering actions emerge in successive cycles as a result of this learning.

Implementation of the Guiding Direction

The Plenary Review guiding direction provides a framework within which subsequent legislation or policy enactments would operate. The guiding direction is not intended to limit—but rather to inform future policy enactments. Much as a fiscal note is required by many legislative assemblies, all subsequent statutory enactments within a policy arena would be required specifically to refer to the relevant Plenary Review direction. Plenary Review requires no enforcement other than reference to the guiding direction. The direction can be modified at any time, but only with the requirement that specific

CONDUCT AND OPERATION 133

consideration be given to the guiding direction and the rationale given for modification. The guiding direction largely accomplishes the Plenary Review intent to consider the consequences, take the broad view, deliberate future requirements, and prescribe general guidelines. The benefit is from the anticipatory thinking, not in an end product which must be rigidly enforced without modification.

Plenary Review will require interpretation and application, as all laws and directions do. Plenary Review would in the first instance provide its own interpretations in successive cycles and obviate the need for much executive or judicial interpretation, to use the federal level as an example. It would, of course, be subject to both judicial and executive interpretation—again, as current law already is. Because of the guiding direction, the court will have a better sense of Congress for interpreting regular legislation and there would likely be reduced need for judicial reviews. The executive and the subordinate administrative agencies will find the Plenary Review direction to be helpful—as well as limiting—through better specifying legislative intent. Rules, regulations and other administrative actions would also follow within the Plenary Review framework much as they currently work within statutory law, but there would be more guidance for implementing decisions.

Plenary Review may well result in making administration more accountable, while at the same time giving it greater flexibility. Administration would be made more accountable through guiding directions specifying intent and providing ultimate criteria for evaluation. On the other hand, administration would be more flexible and have greater leeway were Congress to focus much more on the general aspects of public policy and leave the more detailed implementation to executive and administrative decisions.

An important point to remember is that all enforcement, interpretation and application eventually feed back into the next Plenary Review in the policy body. The basic Plenary Review concept is that the policy body periodically assesses the consequences of the policy as implemented, notes demands and challenges, and re-adjusts the macro-policy direction. In this way, all enforcement and interpretation—including Plenary Review—would have successive evaluation and adaptation on a regular basis.

HOW TO CONDUCT A PLENARY REVIEW

In the abstract, the elements of Plenary Review usually find agreement. The critical questions are usually about how it might work and whether it is feasible. It is easier to say *why* there should be Plenary Review than *how* it should be done. This chapter has presented a number of operational suggestions for the conduct of Plenary Review. Not all operational concerns have been resolved here, but many of the major elements have been addressed. With respect to the remaining operational questions, two points should be noted. First, it is not intended that all matters be pinned down; there should be flexibility to adjust to different policy bodies and contexts. Second, there is much yet to be developed; this will have to issue from further research and experiences in implementation.

Leaving aside issues of adoption, Plenary Review can be used by most policy bodies. As developed in this chapter, Plenary Review can be conducted by the following operational arrangements.

TABLE 6–1
HOW TO CONDUCT A PLENARY REVIEW

Topic	Operating Element
Authorization	Institute a separate Plenary Review mode using powers inherent to most policy bodies. This may be selected reviews (particularly to start) or a comprehensive process.
General Policy Arenas	Develop a general listing of major policy arenas for review, to insure periodic consideration of all major areas.
Periodic Review	Create a cycle to schedule periodic review of major policy arenas every seven to ten years.
Requirement	Require regular reviews of all major policy arenas.

continued...

CONDUCT AND OPERATION

Specific Policy Arena	Define a policy arena of interacting policies and programs for a specific Plenary Review. Modifications may be made in the arena as stated in the general policy list.
Charge	Assign Plenary Review responsibilities to subordinate units for report and approval in a larger policy body or to the body itself as a committee of the whole.
Stewardship Information	Request stewardship reports from those responsible for implementing policies and programs in the policy arena to understand the administrative rationale and recommendations.
Staff Information	Assign support staff to prepare basic information, data, research and reports to be used in the Plenary Review.
Deliberative Format	Utilize a participative and deliberative format (common to most policy bodies) suited to discussion and judgement of macro policy level concerns.
Required Decision	Require that deliberations end in some decision to enable conclusion and timely action.
Quantitative Resolution	Utilize a quantitative vote to enable the best available decision on purposes, values and other complex issues.
Guiding Direction	Develop a guiding direction for the policy arena which assesses consequences, specifies purposes and ends, and provides guidance to future policy actions (macro-policy).
Implementation	Refer to the guiding direction in all future actions in the policy arena. Modifications can be made in the guiding direction after consideration of the direction and statement of the rationale for deviation.
Continue Cycle	Review policy arenas and their guiding directions on a regular periodic basis and make necessary guiding adjustments.

These same elements can be presented in a simple sequence. Table 6-2 presents these in a succinct overview.

TABLE 6–2
AN OVERVIEW OF PLENARY REVIEW

The establishment of a separate Plenary Review mode

- Listing all major public policy arenas
- Scheduling periodic reviews
- Requiring review and decision

Leads To:

Review of specific public policy arenas

- Utilizing and charging subunits
- Considering stewardship reports, other information and counsel
- Using a deliberative and participative format
- Requiring a decision
- Through quantitative resolution

To Produce:

A guiding direction which

- Assesses consequences, specifies purposes, and establishes guiding macro-policy
- Implemented through reference to the guiding direction in subsequent policy

And the Cycle Continues with Periodic Reviews . . .

The use and operation of Plenary Review will be developed further in the following chapters on Plenary Review applications and adoption.

SEVEN: PLENARY REVIEW HISTORY AND EXPERIMENTS

How does Plenary Review work? How might it be applied? Where is it useful? This chapter will briefly review the development of the concept and its use in experimental settings. Chapter Eight will develop the range of Plenary Review applications and Chapter Nine will discuss use of Plenary Review in the U.S. Congress.

BACKGROUND AND STIMULUS

The background and evolution of Plenary Review provides some insight into its nature and operation. The need for a more adequate evaluation of the consequences of public policy and its implementation was a major concern arising out of the experiences and reflection of Julius (Jay) Stern, a Parkersburg, West Virginia, businessman with a longstanding interest in philosophy and public policy. In Jay Stern, experience with the practice of public policy combined with a lifetime of reading and thinking in public affairs and philosophy. As a teenager with interest in philosophy, he wrote to John Dewey on some of his questions about a possible "fundamental hypothetical truth" (and received a reply suggesting gently that there may be no such thing). After graduating from MIT in engineering and after five years of field and headquarters planning duty in the period of World War II, he felt the need to round out his education by auditing philosophy courses at Harvard and American University.

Later as a banker interested in consumer capital necessities at competitive rates, he encountered a federal regulatory system with a relatively narrow vision. Particularly in the last decade, it seemed to Stern, major changes had been made in the public policy regulating banking without congressional action and without standing back to assess past and prospective consequences and to determine desirable guiding directions. Many interpretations, practices and regulations had accumulated with little reflection from Congress and other bodies on what the outcomes were and where it was all headed. No effective congressional (or other) overview of the consequences had informed or guided regulatory practice. The most important issues at the time were the nature of desirable price competition, the unilaterally forced and irreversible breach of the usury ceilings, and the degree of responsible and competitive innovation open to private management in the public interest. Over the last decade, he has argued that the undebated consequences might lead to crisis in financial institutions. This, of course, has come to pass. On moral principle and in protest of regulatory practice which unilaterally imposed undebated consequences on the polity, Mr. Stern voluntarily deeded his majority interest in the bank to the United States as a donation against the national debt. It was impossible, he felt, to operate the bank in ways beneficial to the polity and in accord with moral and social principles, and donation was the only principled option open to him.

THE EVOLUTION OF THE PLENARY REVIEW CONCEPT

Concern for public policy deliberations led Jay Stern to approach Lawrence Spivak, then editor of *American Mercury*, with the notion of a publication presenting an issue of current concern. There would be a statement of facts and responses from individuals with differing viewpoints. Spivak responded pragmatically to Stern that there was enough confusion in the world, "don't add to it."

The need to evaluate the consequences of public policy was also a major concern which developed in conversations between Jay Stern and Melvin Lasky, editor of the British opinion magazine, *Encounter*.

The pair reviewed an apparent need to consider periodically the political, social, economic, moral and institutional consequences of public policy. Stern developed a descriptive outline of a concept he dubbed "Encounter Congress." The idea was to construct responsible and informed discussion of broad public issues in an informal context (which, however, required that a decision be reached). The evaluative overview of public policy through informed adversarial discussion and decision was intended to add to public discussion and congressional insight. A small body of highly knowledgeable individuals, picked each year, would deliberate a significant question of public policy. The deliberations and decisions would be distributed in the journal *Encounter* for both public interest and possible congressional use each following year.

In these conversations with Lasky, Stern argued that policy review could not focus simply on formal law. Instead, he contended that a form of policy review was necessary which could evaluate the actual consequences of a law as implemented and compare them to the original aims which underpinned its passage. Indeed, in many areas the evolutionary development of interpretations and regulations and the often haphazard amendment of public policies have resulted in consequences that are often not even recognized, let alone planned or coordinated. In the area of banking policy, for example, there have been extensive changes in accepted practices without a thoroughgoing review of their import or impact and without adequate discussion of recurring problems of deep and serious national concern and how these are and are not met by free-market processes alone.

With these discussions as a stimulus, Stern and a number of individuals began to discuss and develop the concept. In addition to various practitioners, legislators and citizens, a small group of scholars at West Virginia University participated in discussions, research and experiments based on the notion. Experimental seminars evaluating public policy and utilizing some of these notions were conducted in graduate classrooms. The term "Encounter Congress" changed to "Public Policy Forums" and eventually to "Plenary Review," in an attempt to reflect more accurately the nature of the policy review being developed.

An important aspect of this history is that Plenary Review has developed through serious discussion, innovative brainstorming and experimentation designed for testing. Because the improvement of public policy is so complex and challenging, Plenary Review was purposely developed in a mode best characterized as creative, learning-by-doing, experimental and reflective. The iterative process of discussion, deliberation and experimentation was intended to stimulate thought and practice. The need provided the focus, while the approach to meeting the need was carefully kept open, tentative and experimental.

PLENARY REVIEW EXPERIMENTS

Over a period of several years, a variety of Plenary Review experiments and projects have been undertaken to test ideas and to stimulate thinking. Efforts have varied widely in length, policy focus, participants and decision making approach. Some experiments have employed the classroom as a laboratory while others have used professional and citizen groups to test various concepts. Since the projects have been important in the development of thinking, they are briefly reviewed here with respect to their contribution to the concept of Plenary Review as it has developed.

Discussions on the need for Plenary Review stimulated the idea of creating a group to review a selected policy area. A special "Encounter Congress" seminar was organized in the Department of Public Administration at West Virginia University under the direction of David Williams. About twenty graduate students in Public Administration and Political Science were recruited for a two-day seminar. The seminar was modeled after a legislative committee with the students playing assigned roles (of the Senate Committee reviewing the acid rain provisions of the Clean Air Act). Experts, representing many different views and many of whom had testified before Congress, came before the Committee for statements and questions. The committee then debated and developed its recommendations for congressional revision of the Clean Air Act.

The post-test indicated a great amount of learning in the participants—and they rated the experience very highly. Reviews of this first experiment surfaced two major concerns. First, the broader view appeared to be inadequately developed. The assessment of economic, moral, social, political and institutional consequences often got lost in detail and political skirmishing. Second, although the political interaction worked well (senatorial roles were assigned), rational decision making appeared to be limited. The retrospective view of the professor is that the pluralistic decision process will always be both

History and Experiments

enriched and limited by such factors, but at the time there was concern for a "rational" decision process adequate to meet the challenges of the polity.

Attempting the Rational Decision

Growing out of the concern for a more rational decision process, a semester-long seminar was then organized under the direction of Gerald Pops and David Williams. In formal meetings one-half day per week for a semester, and in many informal work and discussion groups throughout the week, the seminar participants reviewed the policy area of a public employee relations law for the State of West Virginia. (The State of West Virginia is one of the few states with no public employee relations law; the right to strike, for example, is neither permitted nor denied in statutory law.) In reaction to the very political nature of the earlier experiment, this seminar used a synoptic decision making process, clearly identifying each decision step and requiring participants to complete each before moving to the next. Participants were not allowed to jump to decisions, but had to identify carefully the relevant issues, gather information, determine alternatives, analyze alternatives, and only then make the decision.

The final decisions on the issues of public employee relations were presented to a special invited panel, which included public labor organizers, members of the state legislature, and the President of the State AFL-CIO. The defense of positions and the depth of thought were impressive to the invited guests. The President of the State AFL-CIO remarked that some of the subtle understandings and insights the students were able to achieve in this experimental context had taken him years to master.

The comparison of the pre-test and post-test indicated that most individuals involved in the process did not change positions (for example, on the right to strike), but that they learned a great deal about the issues and the facts in this policy area. Again, participants were exceptionally pleased with the experience. The professors were again concerned that the group was not able to develop adequately the broader view, to understand many contextual implications, and to assess many of the consequences of past and proposed policy positions. The very carefully organized and tightly controlled sequential decision process appeared to hamper interaction and insight. It often appeared to get in the way of analysis and judgement. In such an overly structured process, review of consequences and thorough interaction were seen to be too limited.

Moving Toward a Deliberative Process

Since the synoptic decision approach seemed to be insufficiently effective in developing the broad view, a third experiment was devised to continue the search for a decision format. This third project focused again on a public employee relations law for the State of West Virginia. The specific task was to build on the excellent research, identification of issues and options, and recommendations from the previous semester. A graduate seminar in Public Administration under the direction of Gerald Pops was designed to focus on the broad view, open up deliberation and debate, review the public and political consequences, and agree on a report with recommendations. The general format was similar to a presidential commission. The model resulted, as intended, in considerably greater participant control of discussion and direction.

This third experiment illustrated the benefits of participant control, such as would be the case in a legislative body. More self-direction appeared to improve the Plenary Review focus and the decision making. Review and discussion of this led to a fourth project, a semester-long seminar under David Webber, which would have an instructor as a facilitator but would be largely self-structuring and self-directing toward accomplishment of a selected task. In many respects, the model was similar to a task force. The policy focus was the creation of an economic development bill for the State of West Virginia, a rather ambitious effort.

In addition to review of current economic development efforts and assessment of their past consequences, a specified assignment was to go beyond and develop new ideas and practical prospective proposals which might be useful to decision makers. At the end of the semester, the results were presented in a special meeting to a panel of individuals who had had some experience in this area. Two state legislators (one the chair of a joint legislative economic development committee) and a university vice-president (who had led university efforts in economic development) heard the presentation in the assigned roles of a legislative committee hearing the testimony of experts. They grilled the class members on the concepts and proposals. While there were gaps, the student work was well received. As in all earlier experi-

History and Experiments

ments, student involvement and learning received high praise from students and other participants.

The Role of Expert Input

A recurring issue in many of the Plenary Review development discussions was the role of expert knowledge. Although there was generally good quality of student insight and recommendations, the questions remained: What interaction should there be and what is the most beneficial role of policy experts and administrators in conjunction with legislators?

Outside experts had been involved in all the previous projects, but now a need was seen for greater involvement of all kinds of experts, and in particular, actual program administrators. Another semester experiment was designed to involve such actual administrators and a stewardship report. The particular policy focus was the Urban Development Action Grant program (UDAG). Under the direction of Max Stephenson, a rather ambitious undertaking was designed to include actual federal administrators of the UDAG program under both President Reagan and President Carter, a continuing expert panel representing diverse academic fields and views, and various expert witnesses. The seminar also traveled to Baltimore to talk with officials and review actual projects. The student participants were to interact continually with the experts while remaining in control. Five academic experts from different fields worked with the seminar during the entire semester; they included professors from economics, political science, policy studies and social work. The academic experts presented concept papers, argued positions, and responded to student inquiries as determined by the students themselves. The students also met interactively with the actual federal administrators and other experts.

The UDAG project well illustrated the ability of lay persons (legislators, students, citizens) to become knowledgeable in specific areas and to engage in meaningful discussion and rational or reasonable decisions in the context. Expert input was very useful in informing debate and decision, but the nonexpert participants were able to work well in assessment of consequences and recommendations.

Interaction in Policy Arenas

The experiments and projects to this point contributed richly to many discussions and insights. Some projects had had a relatively narrow focus (UDAG) and others had a broader policy focus (economic development). The importance of the policy focus became quite clear in the UDAG project. Some foci (such as UDAG) were too narrow and precluded the comparison of alternative and related programs; other foci were too broad. The "policy arena" concept emerged, as a focus broader than a program but not so broad as to be unmanageable. A sixth project developed experience with the policy focus by sketching the possibilities of rural development as a policy arena. This project included the use of a stewardship report as well as substantial group self-direction.

All the Plenary Review experiments were well-received in the classroom. Students found these experiences to be very beneficial. Many reported that for the first time in their academic careers they were excited by investigation and scholarship. From all reports and tests, student self-direction and investigation into policy arenas appeared to be excellent pedagogical experiences. Faculty also expressed their satisfaction with such a different pedagogical approach.

Development of Plenary Review in Non-Student Groups

The use of Plenary Review in the classroom was very successful as a teaching approach and very useful to thinking through and developing the Plenary Review concept. However, since the classroom is only a limited approximation, it was decided to try the Plenary Review approach outside the university. Barbara and David Webber coordinated two projects.

The West Virginia League of Women Voters had selected the topic of municipal annexation as their focus issue for the coming year. For various reasons, this is an important topic in the State of West Virginia and the League was preparing to discuss the topic towards development of their position on the issue. The League was approached with the idea of using the Plenary Review format over two days to deliberate and develop a position. In the meeting, the Plenary Review concept was presented, a background report gave basic information on the topic, and experts (both national and state) were brought in to be resources for the discussion. Again, participants had almost full control in directing their discussion and in their use of experts. Without reviewing all the details, it can be reported that the experiment went very well. Participants were very pleased with the experience and the practical outcome of the discussion. Academic observers found the process to work well in terms of group dynamics, decision processes and usable knowledge.

With the success of this first test, a second nonacademic experiment was initiated. A statewide conference was organized to which local government practitioners were invited to spend two days in a Plenary Review format on the same topic of municipal annexation. The practitioner involvement again illustrated that Plenary Review can invigorate discussion and provide a perspective which can improve policy review.

The next experiment used a graduate seminar on economic development to reaffirm participant direction and the development of practical policy proposals for future guidance and action. Under the direction of Max Stephenson, the class prepared a report on guiding purposes for the policy arena.

After the series of Plenary Review experiments and the extensive discussions which accompanied them, a draft manuscript was prepared by David Williams to describe and present the Plenary Review concept. Another Plenary Review seminar was organized with two purposes in mind. First, the Plenary Review concept and manuscript was reviewed and debated for about half of the semester. Second, the remainder of the semester was devoted to a Plenary Review of guiding principles for Social Security and related policies. (Senator Moynihan had raised various issues about the Social Security trust fund.) The seminar also experimented with the various elements of Plenary Review (consequences, macro-policy, etc.) as a framework for their discussion and decision.

Plenary Review was developed through the variety of discussions and experiments described above. The process of development is summarized in Table 7-1.

TABLE 7-1
PLENARY REVIEW DEVELOPMENT

- **Conceptual Development**: Stern (with Lasky) outlined an "Encounter Congress" to review periodically economic, social, moral, political and institutional consequences of public policy.

- **Experiential Development**: Seminar on Clean Air Act simulated a legislative committee to test Encounter Congress concepts.

- **Conceptual Development**: Limited macro-policy view and assessment of consequences appeared to require a better decision process.

- **Experiential Development**: Seminar on public employee relations law used a synoptic decision process, carefully going through sequential decision steps.

- **Conceptual Development**: Review indicated that the synoptic decision process hampered deliberation and broad judgement.

- **Experiential Development**: A deliberative format (modeled on a presidential commission) was used to investigate public employee relations law.

- **Conceptual Development**: Greater participant control appeared to improve deliberation, assessment of consequences, broader view and decision.

- **Experiential Development**: Seminar used a task force model (self-structuring and self-directing) to create an economic development bill for West Virginia.

- **Conceptual Development**: The deliberative format appeared to work more effectively. Concern focused on information, expert input and review of administrative practice.

- **Experiential Development**: Seminar analyzed UDAG with stewardship report, expert panel and information base.

- **Conceptual Development**: The deliberative format appeared to work well, but the focus raised concerns. Concept of policy arena was developed.

- **Experiential Development**: Seminar defined a policy arena in rural development and used the deliberative format.

History and Experiments

- **Conceptual Development**: Extensive discussions better described the elements in Plenary Review, particularly the process and decision elements.

- **Experiential Development**: The Plenary Review approach was tested in nonstudent groups; WV League of Women Voters and a municipal officials conference used the arena of annexation.

- **Conceptual Development**: Further discussions developed the elements of Plenary Review and investigated applications beyond legislative bodies.

- **Experiential Development**: Seminar on economic development tested Plenary Review elements, particularly a report assessing the arena and providing guiding principles.

- **Conceptual Development**: The development of a manuscript helped focus discussion of the Plenary Review concept. A retreat reviewed and developed the concept.

- **Experiential Development**: A seminar on Social Security used the latest iteration of the Plenary Review elements, particularly developing a guiding direction.

- **Conceptual Development**: A series of interviews with legislative officials and scholars tested and developed the concepts. A retreat was held to review the manuscript presentation of the Plenary Review concept.

- Discussions and experiments are continuing to hone the Plenary Review concept and its presentation.

In addition to the classroom and other experiments, there have been a number of other activities and efforts. Two retreats were held to debate and develop aspects of the Plenary Review concepts. The retreats included persons who had organized the experiments as well as other scholars, practitioners (including the former Speaker of the House of Delegates in West Virginia) and persons from the Interactivity Foundation (which funded these efforts). A number of individuals were interviewed to further test the concept and collect additional ideas. Interviewees included legislative officials from a number of states, scholars from various universities and people at the Brookings

Institution and the Library of Congress. In a related effort, Gerald Pops and Max Stephenson used many Plenary Review concepts in making linkages between the policy process and dispute resolution and mediation. Working with the National Institute for Dispute Resolution, they published a two-volume work entitled *Conflict Resolution in the Policy Process*. They have also published an article on "Conflict Resolution Methods and the Policy Process" in *Public Administration Review* (Pops and Stephenson, 1989). David Webber has used many of the concepts in various conferences and projects in the Office of Public Policy Resources at the University of Missouri. David Williams, Max Stephenson and David Webber have published an article on Plenary Review in the classroom, "Teaching the Missing Pieces of Policy Analysis," in *PS* (Williams, Stephenson and Webber, 1991).

LEARNING BY DOING

As illustrated in the report on the various experiments and projects, Plenary Review has not been developed in a deliberately planned research design, with explicit testing of each of the various elements. Instead, the several experiments were attempts to apply and experience various notions coming out of discussions. They often served as prelude to other thoughts and as the stimulus to various insights. The process has recognized the fragility of many ideas, the need for gestation and development, the necessity for various iterations and the importance of creative thought. A favorite phrase of Stern—learning by doing—came to characterize much of the development of Plenary Review. The major insights which issued from this process of learning by doing are the following.

First, the format and process used in decision making are important and can influence the decision. Of course, this is not startling information in the decision making literature, but the practical understanding of this led to interesting experiences and insights. Much of the classroom experience suggested that students and lay participants can do much better than often thought if they are given responsibility for learning, directing and deciding. It was often very difficult for the professors to "let go," establish student responsibility and control, and get out of the way of the process while remaining a contributor. The more open and participant-controlled discussion and decision formats appeared to contribute to the overview, participant ownership and judgements of consequences.

Second, the scope of the policy arena appears to be critical in making trade-off judgements. The policy arena can be too narrowly defined or too broadly defined. The former precludes seeing alternative and related efforts which contribute to the policy arena; the latter gives too little focus and depth.

Third, the Plenary Review experiments have shown that relatively uninformed individuals can, through a systematic and yet adaptive process, come to meaningful evaluations and rational judgements (at least as assessed by experts in the area and by professors with some knowledge of the policy issues). Individuals who are not experts can grasp the major issues and outcomes and interact with experts to make meaningful assessments. The quick advances in knowledge to understand and debate the subtleties of policy arenas have often been remarkable. An almost universal experience has been the exhilaration and involvement of all participants. Post-tests have reported substantial learning. Participant reports have been overwhelmingly positive that this was a useful experience. The experience with Plenary Review projects suggests rather strongly that legislators, citizens and students can play an important part in public policy analysis and evaluation. It may bode well for democracy to find that nonexperts have the ability to comprehend rather quickly the critical points and make reasoned judgements.

Fourth, Plenary Review has shown itself to be an overwhelming success as a pedagogical approach. The application to Congress and public policy concerns has yet to be fully assessed, but in the classroom the perspective and format have worked well. The Plenary Review classroom experiments have developed a policy review teaching model which gives insight into important elements often overlooked in more traditional models.

A final generalization comes from the repeated success of the Plenary Review perspective in citizen education and involvement. In statewide applications and in classroom experiences, individuals report great benefit in discussion of policy issues through the Plenary Review approach.

Eight: Plenary Review Applications

Plenary Review is applicable to public policy bodies at all levels and in a wide variety of settings. Plenary Review can make these bodies more effective and add a dimension of policy review now missing. Plenary Review is useful where there is a need to: 1) assess the consequences of past policy actions; 2) broaden evaluations to include longer-term social, moral, political, economic and institutional concerns; 3) deliberate general purposes and guiding principles; and 4) take effective adaptive action. These applications can range from legislatures to executive use, from formal policy bodies to citizens interested in a public policy area, and from the national Congress to the city council. This chapter applies Plenary Review to a wide variety of situations. The next chapter develops the application to the U.S. Congress in greater detail.

Types of Plenary Review Applications

The wide variety of applications of the Plenary Review concept can be distilled into three basic types: legislative applications, managerial applications and citizen applications. Legislative applications include legislative and policy bodies at all levels. Management applications include executive use in governmental, corporate and non-profit organizations. Citizen applications include citizen forums and classroom utilization. These general types, which will be discussed in the chapter, are summarized in Table 8–1.

Table 8-2 illustrates some of the organizations which can use Plenary Review. It also shows that Plenary Review can be used in varying degrees. In some applications, policy analysis and review can 1) end with the identification of the problem and the development of information and options. In other cases, 2) policy may be deliberated, advantages and disadvantages compared and a recommendation made. In still other cases, 3) the deliberation and decision may be followed by empowered and responsible action—that is, review with plenary action and guidance for future policy action. Each of these may be appropriate for different organizations and circumstances.

Plenary Review is most effective, of course, when a policy body is able to identify, develop, deliberate and enact a guiding direction. Unless responsible action follows on review, much of the effectiveness and insight of the evaluation is lost. However, there is still benefit to simply using the Plenary Review perspective to approach and understand a problem or to deliberate and select a preferred option. For example, Congress might use the Plenary Review approach for insight into minimum wage policy; this would enrich debate and decision without enacting a formal guiding direction or establishing a Plenary Review system.

Many organizations and situations limit the degree to which Plenary Review may be applied. For example, a citizen forum can only use Plenary Review to debate and recommend directions for welfare policy. A task force may not have power to implement their guiding direction for juvenile crime. A college seminar may only be able to use Plenary Review to debate environmental policy, assess consequences, and note competing options and indicate a preference. The use of Plenary Review can be beneficial, even though limited, in all degrees of application.

TABLE 8–1
GENERAL PLENARY REVIEW TYPES

Dimension	Legislative Plenary Review	Management Plenary Review	Citizen Plenary Review
Areas of Application	Congress, state legislatures, city councils, advisory boards and other policy bodies	Elected officials, public agencies, corporate and other hierarchical organizations	Commissions, task forces, citizen forums, public interest panels, and classrooms
Objective	To improve public policy through periodic assessment and guidance	To improve organizational policies through periodic assessment and guidance	To improve public policy insight and to increase participation
Format	Separate mode from current policy process	Separate mode from hierarchical process	Created for each review
Periodic Review	Regular review of all arenas	Regular review of all arenas	Selective, not comprehensive
Review of Consequences	Review of past and future consequences of public policy and practice	Review of past and future consequences of organizational policy and practice	Review of past and future consequences of public policy and practice
Action Follow Through	Passage of legislation and oversight of executive implementation	Implementation by executive direction and hierarchical oversight	Advisory only; impact through recommendations and public support
Condition for Adoption	Possible, but may require experience and political incentives	Possible, but will require executive action to establish	Possible, but will require a sponsor or initiator to establish
Policy Arena	Groupings of related public policies and programs, large number	Groupings of related policies and operations, more limited number	Selected for each review, single focus
Process Facilitation	Legislative control, use of regular system for debate and decision	Separate deliberative process, may use facilitator	Deliberative process, need for sponsor or facilitator to initiate.

TABLE 8-2
DEGREES OF PLENARY REVIEW APPLICATION

Using Organization	Problem Development	Deliberation & Recommendation	Deliberation & Action
LEGISLATIVE PLENARY REVIEW			
U.S. Congress	Applicable	Applicable	Applicable
State Legislature	Applicable	Applicable	Applicable
City Councils	Applicable	Applicable	Applicable
Public Boards	Applicable	Applicable	Appl/Not Appl
MANAGEMENT PLENARY REVIEW			
Public Executive	Applicable	Applicable	Appl/Not Appl
Corporate	Applicable	Applicable	Appl/Not Appl
Other Organizations	Applicable	Applicable	Appl/Not Appl
CITIZEN PLENARY REVIEW			
Citizen Forum	Applicable	Applicable	Not Applicable
Classroom	Applicable	Applicable	Not Applicable

PLENARY REVIEW IN LEGISLATIVE AND PUBLIC POLICY BODIES

Plenary Review is particularly designed for the United States Congress and legislative bodies at the state and local levels. Plenary Review will provide these bodies a complementary, reflective decision mode to review systematically the outcomes of past public policies and to discern better future directions and guiding adjustments. The resulting macro-policy in this mode will help legislatures link past actions and future needs. Legislatures face tremendous challenges;

they need such an approach to move to the level of understanding equal to the challenges.

How can a city council steer a city rather than just navigate crisis to crisis? How can a state legislature function as a "double-loop" to make certain the policies and programs of that state support the ends desired? How can Congress be more effective in the organic adaptation of the polity to its challenges? In Plenary Review, a legislature would regularly stand back to take stock. They would step out of the particulars to generalize the impact of past and prospective action. In Plenary Review, the national Congress, state legislatures, city councils and other legislative bodies will regularly review each major policy arena every seven or ten years for appropriate and timely steering action.

How is Plenary Review done in a legislature? The U.S. Congress is a prime application which requires an extensive presentation. Chapter Seven will discuss how Plenary Review might operate in the procedures and structure of Congress. The application of Plenary Review in a state legislature will be similar to Congress because they both have basically similar committee structures, procedures and staff resources. This chapter will apply Plenary Review to smaller legislatures and public policy bodies.

Plenary Review in smaller policy bodies, such as a city council, may be easier to accomplish than Plenary Review in larger bodies for two reasons. First, most city councils are of the size where discussion and decision work well in the body as a whole. A city council can establish a complementary mode to assess general policy arenas and establish directions as a committee of the whole. Second, the range of policies is often more circumscribed. Table 8-3 suggests how a city council can conduct a Plenary Review.

Although a fully developed Plenary Review process can contribute a great deal to the effectiveness of a public policy body, the full application is not needed to obtain some benefit. As noted in Table 8-2, a Plenary Review perspective can enrich policy deliberations in the regular format absent a second separate mode. Indeed, many public policy bodies may gradually incorporate Plenary Review elements in discussing policy issues and in comparing options before adoption of the full-blown process. This, in turn, may lead to a few more city councils or legislative committees demonstrating that Plenary Review can contribute to legislative effectiveness and to wider adoption of Plenary Review.

TABLE 8-3
PLENARY REVIEW IN A CITY COUNCIL

How to Conduct Plenary Review in a City Council:

- Establish a separate Plenary Review mode, listing policy arenas and scheduling periodic review.
- Select a policy arena for review. (Absent a general system, Plenary Review can start with this step.)
- Collect stewardship reports and other basic information.
- Use a deliberative format to discuss the policy arena consequences and purposes.
- Make decision by quantitative vote.
- Adopt a guiding direction which assesses consequences and establishes macro-policy for future actions in the policy arena.
- Refer to the guiding direction in subsequent policy actions.

There are other bodies with policy-making responsibility in addition to legislatures where Plenary Review might apply. These are most often formal and empowered, but other times they are informal and advisory. These include policy boards, advisory committees, boards of review, commissions and boards of directors. The Plenary Review macro-perspective and review of outcomes allies closely with the mission of policy boards. In the cases where a board has formal responsibility and power to direct the organization, the application of Plenary Review would be very similar to the legislative application discussed above. In the cases where boards and committees are advisory, there is the same potential benefit to provide insight about consequences of social, moral, economic and political relevance, to understand policy as practiced, to determine purposes and to propose appropriate steering action. The difference lies solely in the degree of sovereign power to implement authoritative decisions.

PLENARY REVIEW IN MANAGEMENT APPLICATIONS

The Plenary Review approach is also useful to elected public executives, administrative agencies, private sector managers and non-profit organizations. The objective of Plenary Review in management applications is to improve organizational policies and executive actions through periodic assessment of consequences and appropriate guidance. Plenary Review provides a broader perspective now often missing in the press of demands on executives. Application to various management contexts will be made in the following sections.

Public Management Plenary Review

The objective for a public executive in utilizing the Plenary Review approach is to improve policy making and management through assessing the whole rather than always being enmeshed in the administrative parts. It is an attempt to meet and adjust to the environment of the organization and thereby increase organizational effectiveness.

Plenary Review should be a separate decision format periodically used by the executive staff to review major policy arenas. As desired, Plenary Review deliberations might be enriched and extended by participation of other agency staff, advisory groups and clientele groups. Plenary Review can also take place in more limited applications. It can simply be a perspective within the mind of the elected or appointed public executive useful in guiding a public organization or it can be a format for an executive retreat to understand trends and goals.

How is Plenary Review conducted in public management applications? The level and unit to conduct Plenary Review must be determined. It could be a governor's cabinet on children's issues covering a number of departments. It might be the executive staff of the Department of Highways reviewing a major program responsibility. It could be the management team of a Job Service office discussing issues appropriate at that level of responsibility. Plenary Review in public agencies must recognize the hierarchical nature of administration. Plenary Review may be solely executive level review, but it could also utilize the hierarchical levels for reviews appropriate to each level of authority. Policy arenas at the lower levels can be assessed at that level, incorporated in a Plenary Review at the next level, and so forth. For example, it might be appropriate to perform a Plenary Review at the bureau level, then at the office or administration level, and finally the department level. Or, a city streets unit could do a Plenary Review, which is then incorporated in the public works department Plenary Review, which is then summarized in a Plenary Review by the city manager for ultimate review by the city council. Follow-through

PLENARY REVIEW APPLICATIONS 157

is often simplified because hierarchical direction can be used to implement decisions. In this way, Plenary Review can serve as a periodic review of policy and practice.

Germane policies and operations are grouped into arenas, although the number of policy arenas would likely be less than that in a legislative application. It continues to be important to identify policy arenas which extend beyond the individual agency. For example, a program assigned to the Department of Labor may be intertwined with a program in the Department of Health and Human Services, or both programs may focus on the same general need but be administratively separate. These interrelationships are important to identify and understand even through coordination cannot be established at that level.

Steps in conducting Plenary Review in a public management setting are listed in Table 8-4.

The Plenary Review process is readily applicable to a legislature where deliberation and voting can expand creative considerations and then establish closure through a voting process. Open discussion and deliberation are often more difficult to achieve in a hierarchical setting. While any hierarchical use of the Plenary Review perspective could be of some benefit, it is more effective to conduct this review in a format conducive to reflection and deliberation. A retreat setting, a facilitator or various deliberative formats might be used for this purpose. Techniques from group dynamics can be used to open the process, expand interaction, encourage creativity, enhance refining of ideas, minimize dominant personalities and compensate for group limitations. The following paragraphs note some of the techniques which may be used.

The Delphi Technique attempts to get around the limitations of face-to-face group interaction, particularly in an hierarchical context, while extending group judgement. It solicits and compares anonymous judgements on a topic through sequential questionnaires interspersed with information and feedback of opinions from earlier responses. The Nominal Group Technique also attempts to minimize the disadvantages of group dynamics and face-to-face interaction. The technique uses a structured group meeting without discussion. The ideas and points which are made (usually on note cards or flip charts) are run through a number of cycles with persons reacting and refining. These techniques can be used with Plenary Review if desired to open up deliberations, to consider all views, to reduce the control of a few participants, to increase the depth of participation or to form the base for further discussion.

TABLE 8–4
PLENARY REVIEW IN PUBLIC AGENCIES

How to Conduct Plenary Review in a Public Agency:

- Establish a separate Plenary Review mode, listing policy arenas and scheduling periodic review; the separate mode should be non-hierarchical.
- Select a policy arena for review at the level of authority. (Absent a general system Plenary Review can start here.)
- Collect stewardship reports and other basic information through hierarchical and staff lines.
- Use a deliberative format to discuss the policy arena, best done through a non-hierarchical process, facilitators may be helpful.
- Assess consequences, identify guiding purposes, integrate related policies in a broader perspective.
- Make decision by quantitative vote, subject to hierarchical approval.
- Adopt a guiding direction which establishes macro-policy.
- Implement changes and actions through hierarchical direction.
- Refer to the guiding direction periodically.

The MAUT-Bayesian technique offers a structured process through which goals are first identified and ranked and then alternative strategies are compared through identifying those which maximize the goals. It is simply a structured way to identify, compare and compute the options and goals using the judgements of the participants. The goals and alternative strategies are related in a matrix and Bayesian statistics are used so that subjective discussions and evaluations of goals and strategies can be rationalized. The MAUT-Bayesian approach can help to analyze and compare goals and strategies in a Plenary Review format.

Principled bargaining techniques might also be applied to the Plenary Review format. This approach stems from the Harvard negotiation project (reported in Fisher and Ury, *Getting to Yes: Negoti-*

ating Agreement Without Giving In). It requires that discussion focus on principles and interests rather than positions, that objective criteria and goals be set before moving to specifics, that creative and broad thinking be the beginning point for all discussion, that participants attempt to invent options for mutual gain, that decisions be based on standards and criteria rather than force of will or parliamentary rules which avoid issues and that questions be framed to elicit an overall perspective. Although there are significant differences, there are important resemblances to Plenary Review notions of macro-policy, guiding purposes, assessment of consequences, broader perspective and deliberative format.

There are a myriad of other policy review techniques which focus on public management concerns. Techniques which coordinate programs and budgets include program budgeting, PPBS (planning-programming-budgeting system) and ZBB (zero-base budgeting) (Swiss, 1991). Many states and other jurisdictions have established futures commissions, strategic planning, policy task forces and a variety of policy planning processes (Benveniste, 1989). These all have benefits and each overlaps some particulars of Plenary Review. At the same time, none of these are incompatible with Plenary Review. A variety of formats and processes can be used to assess consequences, integrate policy areas, deliberate guiding principles and propose action.

One last variant should be noted after the discussions of legislative and public management Plenary Review. The two might be connected in one system. Plenary Review of a policy arena might rise through various administrative levels, be evaluated by the chief executive and then be transmitted to the legislature as the basis for their own review. For example, job training programs might be assessed at various levels of responsibility. The Plenary Review of an agency task force might feed into a governor's cabinet for broader deliberation and then be submitted to the legislature for committee and floor review. The guiding direction approved by the legislature then guides legislative, executive and administrative actions in that policy arena. Each level has a different scope and responsibility which adds to the process. Legislative and managerial reviews can complement one another in a continuing sequence.

Another approach which combines the executive and the legislature in Plenary Review is to have one Plenary Review group include representatives of each. Such a focus could be given formal power or it could be advisory. For example, the State of Illinois used a similar mechanism to review major issues in health care. The focus group was chaired by the Lieutenant Governor and included key legislative leaders, state health officials and representatives from physician, hospitals and other health provider groups. The general principles developed then provided guidance to legislative and executive actions.

In summary, Plenary Review in the executive branch will help public managers conceptualize and assess the mission and performance of the agency. Plenary Review can be an organizational mechanism for planning, orientation and adaptation. It adds the general view and the outcome perspective to the busy detail of administrative operations. Better insight into consequences, attempts to discern directions, coordination of policy arenas and deliberation of general guidelines within the statutory mandate will improve policy making and administrative direction.

Corporate Plenary Review

The application of Plenary Review to corporate and other private organizations has been prefigured in the previous section. While this application will not be the focus of this book, it should be noted that Plenary Review can be insightful for private sector executives and boards of directors. As it periodically assesses the general consequences of past performance, determines desired outcomes and directs subsequent efforts, Plenary Review will improve corporate policies and orientation. Taking stock and steering the system leads to leadership, as opposed to being mired in management details. It is critical for private sector organizations, which are particularly dependent on the context and their customers for survival, to assess the relationship with the environment and determine necessary adaptations. An organization may otherwise grow in directions opposite to the trends in its environment and find itself in crisis. For example, Plenary Review may have helped avert many of the crises that arose in banking, investment and junk bond financing as managers better noted consequences and considered a broader perspective. Plenary Review is basic to market responsiveness as well as internal organizational performance.

Steps in conducting Plenary Review in a private corporation setting are listed in Table 8-5.

Policy coherence and assessment of results can be as critical in situations where the "bottom line" of profit controls as in more service-oriented public sector organizations. It is equally important that the assessment of consequences in the private sector organization go beyond the criterion of profit to include assessment of the social, moral, political, economic and institutional consequences. This is argued for three reasons. First, these consequences influence profitability through public perception, organizational acceptance, public image, desirability of product and support of the organization. Second (and making assertions without discussing the long debates on this topic), the private sector has a social responsibility as an integral and interdependent part of the collective. Third, private sector responsiveness to social, moral, political, economic and institutional concerns partially determines public sector actions. Regulation is often a public response to corporate unresponsiveness to these elements; so, if these factors are not considered internally, then public institutions may consider them and establish controls.

TABLE 8-5
PLENARY REVIEW IN PRIVATE CORPORATIONS

How to Conduct Plenary Review in a Private Corporation:

- Establish a separate Plenary Review mode, listing policy arenas and scheduling periodic review; the separate mode should be non-hierarchical.

- Select a policy arena for review at the level of authority. (Absent a general system Plenary Review can start here.)

- Collect stewardship reports and other basic information through hierarchical and staff lines.

- Use a deliberative format to discuss the policy arena, best done through a non-hierarchical process, facilitators may be helpful.

- Assess consequences, identify guiding purposes, integrate related policies in a broader perspective.

- Make decision by quantitative vote, subject to hierarchical approval.

- Adopt a guiding direction which establishes macro-policy.

- Implement changes and actions through hierarchical direction.

- Refer to the guiding direction periodically.

Plenary Review in Non-Profit Organizations

The Plenary Review decision process can also meet many needs of non-profit organizations. These include public but non-governmental organizations, labor unions, associations, professional groups, employee associations, employer associations, charitable organizations, religious organizations, taxpayer groups and so forth. Because the existence of many of these organizations is frequently tenuous and because many are constituent based, these organizations need a grasp on needs and demands, a responsiveness to the environment, and an ability to adapt. Plenary Review, as both a perspective and an approach, can assist organizations to accomplish these matters.

Plenary Review may also be used as a mechanism through which the constituents can participate and through which the organization can build support. Plenary Review can be used by the governing board to review major policy arenas and establish guiding direction, but Plenary Review can also be used with various groups and individuals to deliberate policy issues and recommend options. For example, a labor union might periodically sponsor a retreat to develop major labor-management issues and possibilities. Such a discussion might involve local leaders, management representatives and various related groups. Plenary Review can contribute to these other organizations in the same manner it can be of benefit to public and corporate organizations.

CITIZEN USE OF PLENARY REVIEW

One of the most interesting applications of Plenary Review is its use in various citizen forums. While the use of Plenary Review in policy bodies and legislatures is still conjecture, citizen applications is one area where there is some limited experience. Citizen groups can deliberate various policy arenas for the benefit of both themselves and public policy (particularly as the rationale and conclusions receive attention by policy makers). Citizen applications can range from national commissions assessing the consequences of banking policy to local groups assessing general directions in zoning. They can range from discussions of college students or lay participants to the lucubrations of experts.

Plenary Review in Citizen Forums

Plenary Review may serve well as a format for public debates, national commissions, citizen forums, think tank discussions and public interest organization projects. In this usage, Plenary Review is intended to improve the insight, discussion and outcome of the public policy debate. As noted in Table 8-2, this application is limited by the lack of power to take action and to directly use the guiding direction. On the other hand, the assessment of consequences, the macro-policy perspective and the determination of general public purposes are well suited to citizen uses. Because they are external to the process, citizens in a Plenary Review mode can frequently stand back, make assessments, see trends, note assumptions, and suggest corrections which might escape those enmeshed in the legislative or executive process.

In the experiments used to develop the Plenary Review concept, two different citizen forums were utilized. In one application, a state-wide meeting of the League of Women Voters used the Plenary Review format to discuss and develop a position on an important state issue. In the second application, local officials from across the state deliberated the same topic in a Plenary Review format. (Chapter Seven reviews in more detail the Plenary Review experiments.)

Citizen Plenary Review is also a worthwhile endeavor for the purposes of citizen education and participation. Plenary Review can enable citizens to think more broadly and systematically about public policy consequences and alternative actions. The process can inform citizens while confronting the issues involved in analyzing a policy problem. Plenary Review is an excellent format through which citizens can participate as part of their civic role.

The Plenary Review requirement for a decision is particularly important in citizen forums because it produces an action focus not just analysis. This helps distinguish the Plenary Review format from general public forums. The decision focus is critical to convert discussants to realistic decision makers. Practicality and motivation to participate are stimulated by the knowledge that there will have to be closure on a joint decision. Participants are made more responsible decision makers when a decision is required.

Decisions in a citizen Plenary Review are based on their own knowledge, values and beliefs and what technical information they can glean from additional information such as stewardship reports and consultation with officials and experts. Plenary Review members will test emerging insights and arguments against each other and these other sources of information. The result will be a blend of ordinary and specialized analytic knowledge. This is not greatly different from what any legislative body brings to and utilizes in review and decision. The product will not be the "perfect" answer to meet all contingencies and perspectives. It will simply be the accumulated wisdom of that group resulting from that process. It will offer insight and information—perhaps even creative insight and new information—to a policy arena. This should be seen not as a final product, but as one step in the refining process in that policy arena. The conclusion of a citizen forum is, of course, merely advisory; it will not have the force of law. At the same time, the force of its rationale and recommendations can influence policy makers and support further citizen action.

How is a citizen forum conducted in the Plenary Review format? What steps must be arranged? Table 8-6 identifies the steps in a citizen Plenary Review.

TABLE 8–6
PLENARY REVIEW IN A CITIZEN FORUM

How to Conduct Plenary Review in a Citizen Forum:

- Initiate by a sponsoring organization or group, which will usually select the topic.
- Recruit and organize participants, ranging from citizen groups to expert panels.
- Collect basic information, agency reports and expert input.
- Use a deliberative format to discuss the policy arena and serve as a facilitator as necessary.
- Use Plenary Review elements to frame discussion.
- Come to a decision by quantitative vote.
- Recommend a guiding direction which assesses consequences, analyzes guiding principles and suggests policy actions.
- Publicize policy analysis and recommended guiding direction.

Plenary Review in the Classroom

The Plenary Review format has also been used as an innovative approach to teach public policy analysis in the classroom. While it can function much the same way as the citizen forum in reviewing policy arenas and providing an input into policy discussions, the Plenary Review perspective can contribute to policy studies in the classroom in ways otherwise difficult to achieve. The most difficult pieces of policy analysis to teach are 1) the feel for the responsibility and pressures of the decision maker, 2) an overview of the broad social, economic, political, institutional and moral consequences of policies, 3) the difficulty of selecting and implementing some action, and 4) an understanding of policy as both the formal enactment and subsequent implementing rules and interpretations. Because these practical and real life concerns are difficult to teach, they are often missing from many courses and seminars.

A series of experimental seminars at West Virginia University has developed Plenary Review as a classroom approach which allows students to understand better policy development, choice processes and specific policy arenas in more depth than many other methods of teaching policy analysis. (The seminars are reviewed at greater length in Chapter Seven.) Used in the classroom, Plenary Review is a decision-driven process that allows students to become engaged in a broader consideration of an area of public policy, including the multi-faceted consequences and the information available from both academic and governmental sources. Plenary Review encourages participants to look beyond their initial partisan positions by considering the moral, social, economic, political and institutional consequences of policy. Students are encouraged to think broadly, across a range of dimensions, about the consequences of policy choice. This focuses students on the general principles on which a policy is predicated as well as its implementation and performance.

The first part of the course is usually a thoroughgoing, yet quite unstructured, discussion of information from two sources: first, readings, articles, agency reports, performance data and books selected by the instructor, and second, the knowledge, values and beliefs of the student. In many of the classes, a third source of information has come from expert speakers, including both practitioners and academics.

Plenary Review is intended so that the class must arrive at a decision as a result of their review and deliberation. This radically changes the climate and structure of the classroom experience. Students participate in the Plenary Review process on the premise that their collective efforts—as in a legislature—will produce policy decisions. And to complete the simulation, class participants have significant control of the process, organization and timing; they are treated as "responsible decision makers" in the fullest sense of the term. Although many teachers are reluctant to give up full control of discussion content and process, students in these experiments have risen to the responsibility and a stronger commitment to the process and outcome has been engendered as they think in the role of decision makers. Of course, Plenary Review can not guarantee improved policy outcomes—nor can any legislature; however, both students and professors almost unanimously report that the effort does improve the depth and breadth of participants' useable policy knowledge.

Plenary Review in the classroom includes elements common to other applications. Table 8-7 suggests how a classroom Plenary Review can be conducted.

Experience with a variety of approaches suggests that participant control and more open, deliberative formats appear to work better than structured and controlled formats. While it is very helpful for a professor to establish the approach, specify the kind of output, provide basic information, perform staff work and facilitate the details of necessary arrangements, it has worked well for participants to control the interaction, timing and decision process. As experience progressed, less and less control from either the format or teacher was exercised. Students rose well to the challenge of self-direction within the loose framework of the elements of Plenary Review. The relatively unstructured format worked well as the professors gained more courage to relinquish control of the process.

In the seminars, the following points appeared to increase the effectiveness of the Plenary Review approach. First, the professor is best seen as a facilitator rather than in the traditional role. Although the professor organizes and coordinates the course, selects basic readings, and initially fosters discussion and interaction, the key focus must be student interaction and decision.

Second, the students (and the professor) need to develop and focus the public policy arena being investigated. The initial portion of the course should work to develop a common base of information from balanced readings and to identify the basic issues. Third, it is most helpful to expose students to the rationale and consequences of the policy under review from the view of those responsible for the program—a stewardship report from responsible officials on the implementation and performance. This can be accomplished by involving practitioners (as available) in the course or it can be approximated by annual reports, evaluations and other agency information.

**TABLE 8-7
PLENARY REVIEW IN THE CLASSROOM**

How to Conduct Plenary Review in a Classroom:

- Be organized and scheduled by the professor.
- Recruit students by course listing or by invitation.
- Select the policy arena by class action or professor determination.
- Collect information and analysis through student research, professor selection, invited experts and other sources.
- Engage in discussion and deliberation in a relatively open format, generally with student direction and choice.
- Facilitate through the professor as necessary, while being careful not to control the process.
- Use the Plenary Review elements to frame discussion.
- Come to a decision by quantitative vote.
- Recommend a guiding direction in a final report which provides student analysis, discusses options, assesses consequences and suggests guiding purposes.
- Present the final report in the class and to other interested persons as desired.

Fourth, extensive involvement has been a key element. Indeed, the Plenary Review seminar has often been a major learning experience because of the depth of involvement. Students report that for the first time in their academic experiences they have started to accept some responsibility for their own learning and to taste the excitement of intellectual investigation under their own control. Student involvement is critical because it simulates the reality of the discussion and eventual decision. Students act as if they were responsible decision makers as they evaluate a policy and its consequences and come to a decision.

Fifth, the requirement for a collective decision continually focuses student interaction and review (while stimulating realistic involvement). Abstract discussions of policy become transformed into practical issues of applications and outcomes. This sensitizes students to the broad range of alternatives, concerns and dimensions which confront responsible decision-makers. Sixth, the scope of the policy arena studied needs to be carefully selected—it can be too narrow (and overlook alternative and related programs) or too broad (and have too little focus and depth).

Student development and student learning have been important. While students learn a great deal about substantive policies, they also learn to develop and define issues, visualize problems, break issues into component parts, and bring relevant concepts to bear. They learn skills of leadership, interaction and debate. The student role is pro-active rather than passive; many class members have reported Plenary Review to be one of the most engaging intellectual experiences they have had. While there have been some frustrations in the process, students have generally been weaned from dependent roles as readers/gatherers to more mature roles as evaluators/ advocates.

SUMMARY

Plenary Review is useful in a wide variety of applications where it is important to assess the consequences of past policy actions, deliberate guiding purposes and take adaptive action. The three main areas for application of Plenary Review are the following.

- Plenary Review in legislatures and policy bodies can improve outcomes through regular review of policies and their consequences and determination of prospective action.

- Plenary Review can be utilized in public and private executive applications to improve policies, assess consequences, take strategic actions and establish a broad perspective.

- Plenary Review can be utilized in citizen forums and classroom applications to develop policy recommendations and to increase participation and education.

NINE: PLENARY REVIEW IN THE UNITED STATES CONGRESS

The prime application of Plenary Review is to the United States Congress. The challenges to policy making are particularly critical at the national level. Plenary Review will enable Congress to meet many governance responsibilities not now well met. This chapter will describe the potential operation of Plenary Review in Congress.

THE HILL NEEDS HELP

Previous chapters have developed the need for more effective policy leadership. This need is abundantly clear in the performance of Congress. The social, economic, political, moral and institutional consequences of past enactments are not well reviewed on a regular basis. There is rarely coherent, integrated policy which deliberates the interrelationships with other policies and which bases action on consequences and desired ends. Guiding public purposes and macro-policy concerns are infrequently considered. Policy leadership is not adequate to meet many challenges.

One concise evaluation of the need for more effective public policy responses from Congress is presented in a recent book by Michael

Mezey. He developed two categories of criteria for good public policy; democratic criteria focus on responsiveness and accountability, while managerial criteria require that policy be informed, timely, coherent, effective and responsible (Mezey, 1989: 7-9). While Congress responds somewhat to the democratic criteria, Mezey argued that "Congress seems structurally incapable of producing public policy that is informed, timely, coherent, effective and responsible" (Mezey, 1989: 142-143). And viewing the total system, he concluded that the joint presidential-congressional policy process fails "to meet democratic standards and because of its strong bias toward inaction, would also fail to produce policies that would meet managerial standards" (Mezey, 1989: 46). In his view, the current policy system results in policy stalemate or bad public policy. Ripley and Franklin have also concluded that American public policy is slow to change and is unresponsive to general interests (1991: 182).

The need for more effective public policy and a more effective Congress is quite evident even to the casual observer. Survey research shows that Americans are clearly unhappy with congressional performance and that dissatisfaction with Congress has grown dramatically over the last two decades (Ladd, 1990: 58-61). Coverage of Congress in the popular press is generally negative. There are extensive calls for congressional reform (reviewed in Chapter Four). Many are asking whether congressional leadership is still possible (Kornacki, 1990). Given this widespread dissatisfaction, how can Congress become more effective in its public policy responsibilities? Plenary Review is proposed in the following sections as one approach to greatly increase congressional effectiveness.

CONGRESSIONAL PLENARY REVIEW

There are three main options for the conduct of Plenary Review in Congress. First, it can be used as a complementary mode in floor deliberation. Second, it can be used in congressional committees. Third, special committees can be created to perform Plenary Review.

Plenary Review as a Floor Format

Plenary Review may be used on the floor of each chamber of Congress. In this application, Plenary Review would be a regular complementary mode for policy review. Each house of Congress could add this deliberative format to focus better on past and prospective consequences and determine macro-policy. Congress would periodically step out of the normal statutory process into a second mode to deliberate major arenas of public policy. This is similar to the point made by *Washington Post* columnist David Broder when he noted two kinds of issues. Many issues, he said, can be handled in the routine of the legislative process. "But if it were possible to handle just a few big and consequential issues each year...what a boon it would be to our democracy..then it might just be possible for Congress to recover its reputation and for the voters to believe, once again, that the government works for them" (Broder, 1991). All major arenas would be scheduled on a staggered basis every seven or ten years. Plenary Review will not replace current congressional processes; it will be a complement which can guide the current policy process and can add perspectives which are missing.

In the separate Plenary Review mode, each chamber of Congress would deliberate and debate the policy arena at issue. Their deliberations would draw from stewardship reports, data supplied by the responsible administrators and information from the President. In addition, congressional staff analyses and background hearings may be completed as desired and assigned. This information would combine with their own discussions and analysis. In this mode, participants would use the Plenary Review framework to focus on the broader view and the assessment of consequences. As members of Congress evaluate the social, economic, political, moral and institutional consequences of past policy, they will better understand possible outcomes, some of which may or may not be those intended or those desirable. They will note the relationships of related policies. They will ruminate on guiding public purposes. They will debate macro-policy, those generalities which will guide more specific future policy actions. They will attempt to establish more coherent integrated policy through establishing the general public purposes and adopting adaptive actions.

The conventional wisdom has been that little of importance takes place on the floor of Congress, that the floor is mainly for show. It need not be this way and changes may already be in progress. In an important recent book, Steven Smith has argued that during the last three decades, the House and Senate floors have been transformed into "far more important arenas of substantive policy making" (1989: 1). He has documented well the changes toward a more collegial, floor oriented process. Smith's book illustrated "institutional innovation and adaptation to changing conditions" in the Congress (Smith,

1989: 233-235). And, Bach and Smith have shown that the House of Representatives has changed in fundamental ways since the 1960's (1988: vii). Perhaps Plenary Review as a deliberative floor process to evaluate policy may not be too far removed in kind from changes and trends in the last three decades. While it would be a radical change in degree from current procedure, Plenary Review may fit rather than fight these trends. Perhaps more improvement is possible.

On another point, Smith has documented the importance of formal rules in molding behavior and outcomes (Smith, 1989). He and Bach have also noted the influence of special rules (from the House Rules Committee) to shape and influence floor deliberation (Bach and Smith, 1988: 8). Perhaps a Plenary Review format also could be important in influencing the behavior and product of Congress. Establishment of Plenary Review rules and procedures could help define how issues are debated and decided. This will be particularly so in a separate Plenary Review mode, even more so than attempting to incorporate the basic elements of Plenary Review in current processes.

Congressional evaluation of the policy arena would culminate in the enactment of a guiding direction. As a formal enactment of Congress, the guiding direction could either be included with otehr statutory legislation (as a general guiding statement of policy purposes) or could constitute a separate category (perhaps, a category of Plenary Review resolutions). The guiding direction is intended to inform other more specific subsequent policy enactments. Each chamber should require that proposed legislation refer to the guiding direction in the appropriate arena. Further public policy actions would have to be within the guiding direction; however, there should be no hesitation to change the direction as needed. Changes are only required to take the direction specifically into account—the benefit is from the thinking about general purposes, not from rigid enforcement.

The House and the Senate will each enact a guiding direction in the policy arena which has been scheduled. Reconciliation would be handled as in current legislation. After passing either house of Congress, the guiding direction will be considered and approved (or amended) by the other house. Differences will be resolved in conference committee and approved by each chamber. At this point, there are two possibilities depending on whether Plenary Review has been adopted solely in Congress or broadly in the executive-legislative policy process. If Plenary Review is established solely by Congress as a system for its own deliberation, this is the end of the process. Plenary Review as an internal congressional process would provide coordination and enhance policy decisions. If the process includes the executive (developed later in the Chapter), then the guiding direction would be sent to the President. It would be approved or vetoed by the President (and a veto could be overridden). In any event, Plenary Review would be part of the legislative record and would follow most provisions for statutory enactment.

TABLE 9-1
PLENARY REVIEW IN CONGRESS

How to Conduct Plenary Review in Congress:

- Establish a separate mode, list policy arenas and schedule periodic review.
- Select a policy arena for review. (Absent a general system, Plenary Review can start with this step.)
- Charge each body (as a committee of the whole) to complete Plenary Review on an assigned policy arena, or charge committees to complete a Plenary Review and report its findings.
- Collect stewardship reports and other basic information; organize staff support
- Use Plenary Review elements in floor deliberation--assess consequences, integrate related policies, review at the macro-policy level.
- Make decision by quantitative vote.
- Adopt a guiding direction in each house of Congress which assesses consequences and establishes macro-policy for the arena; refer to other house of Congress.
- Reconcile difference in guiding directions in conference committee, approve in each chamber.
- Record guiding direction as a legislative enactment, acknowledge the guiding direction in subsequent policy actions in the arena.
- Enact modifications to the guiding direction as may from time to time be appropriate.

After passage, the guiding direction will guide further congressional actions in that policy arena as well as guide implementation and interpretation in the executive branch and administrative agencies.

Congressional, executive and administrative agencies and officials will have the guiding sense of macro-policy for their actions and programs in a policy arena. As they design operations and fill in the micro-policy of rules and regulations, they will have reference to these guiding directions. The courts will also find the guiding direction useful to determine the sense of Congress as they are called on to interpret the law.

And then the whole process recycles as Congress regularly revisits the policy arena, including earlier guiding directions and their modification in the process of specific enactments, assesses consequences and readjusts guiding purposes. In the Plenary Review format, Congress not only better evaluates and creates public policy, but creates a feedback system where it learns from past efforts and directs future actions.

Plenary Review can be implemented as a second mode of floor deliberation in the House of Representatives and the Senate. Indeed, such an application would be very similar to the original operation of Congress. In the original House, for example, most business was conducted in the committee of the whole where policy was articulated and debated. After agreement was reached on general principles, a select committee was appointed to write the formal bill (Shepsle, 1988: 464-465). These committees had a limited charge and a limited life; they were simply to translate the general will into statutory language. Operating as a committee of the whole, each chamber in essence would form a Plenary Review body.

Plenary Review in Congressional Committees

Although Plenary Review would work well on the floor of each chamber, the use of congressional committees can offer similar analytical benefits and may be easier to adopt and use. The standing committees would receive the Plenary Review assignment for legislative matters in their areas of concern. In turn, subcommittees could be directed to accomplish the Plenary Review for their several policy responsibilities. Plenary Review will help committees and subcommittees to better conceptualize and assess the policy arenas they are assigned. It provides exactly the kind of policy and planning tool needed by each committee or subcommittee.

Committees and subcommittees may be the size for more effective deliberation and decision than the floor of each Chamber of Congress. Since scheduling Plenary Review into an already overcrowded congressional agenda is a major problem, congressional subunits might reserve Plenary Review time or schedule a retreat for Plenary Review (some committees have already used retreats to establish perspective and plan committee operations).

The Plenary Review analysis and guiding direction would then be referred to the next levels. For example, a subcommittee could complete a Plenary Review on science policy. This could be reviewed and amended at the committee level. Committee decisions could then be reviewed and amended by the House or the Senate as a whole. In this way, the bulk of Plenary Review analysis and deliberation could be accomplished at lower levels and referred to higher levels for consideration.

Special Plenary Review Committees

Conference committees, currently used to reconcile legislative actions of the two houses, are another structure suitable to conduct Plenary Review assignments. Adapting the current approach, members from both houses who are most involved in the policy arena (such as committee chairs and policy initiators) would be appointed to this committee. The conference committee would have the specific and limited assignment to conduct a Plenary Review on an assigned policy arena and report back to both houses. Again using current practice, the separate houses of Congress would approve the macropolicy or return it for further consideration.

Special joint committees, which represent both the House and the Senate, can also be used for Plenary Review. These might be standing joint committees or specifically created committees; there could be multiple committees or one Plenary Review joint committee. In recent times, joint budget and economic committees have illustrated the advantages and disadvantages of such an arrangement (see Ellwood, 1985). One example of the general consideration of a major policy arena (but without a Plenary Review decision) was the conference on the new economy co-sponsored by the Joint Economic Committee, the House Committee on Small Business and the Congressional Clearinghouse on the Future (U.S. Congress, Joint Economic Committee, 1984).

Another possibility, which Sundquist has discussed, is a "supercommittee" which would integrate policies and produce a cohesive congressional program (1981: 438). Such a committee was contemplated by the Legislative Reorganization Act of 1946, which provided for a majority and minority policy committee in each house. A supercommittee would lay out the *general* program and policy in advance. Although Sundquist is skeptical about the ability of this concept to work in the current Congress and although Plenary Review would face the same problems, the concept illustrates a possible Plenary Review arrangement.

While it would not incorporate all the elements, many of the functions of Plenary Review might be approximated within the congressional party caucuses. Plenary Review could serve as a device in the caucus to assess consequences of the major policy arenas and develop the macro-policy as a party position. This would give deliberation in the committees and on the floor more meaning and choices would be better clarified for the legislator. This approach does not achieve the full Plenary Review ideal, but it would add to policy debates and inform understanding through regular use of the Plenary Review perspective. These preparatory debates would then inform floor deliberation and action.

STAFF SUPPORTS

Various staff arrangements can be developed to undergird congressional Plenary Review. Plenary Review staff may be attached to committees, subcommittees or individual members of Congress as Plenary Review is conducted in various arrangements. Special Plenary Review committees should have their own staff support. A congressional staff agency may be helpful for scheduling and organizing Plenary Review. Such a staff arm could collect relevant background information, perform preliminary studies and work with the committee or unit conducting the Plenary Review.

Various other organizations might also contribute to the Plenary Review process. Existing congressional staff arms can provide research and information for Plenary Review. These include the General Accounting Office, the Office of Technology Assessment, the Congressional Research Service of the Library of Congress, the Congressional Budget Office and various institutes such as the Congressional Clearinghouse for the Future. Other arrangements are also possible. For example, Frye has called for an Institute for Congress to inform Congress about emerging policy issues and to provide analyses and studies (1976: 274-280).

Implementing Devices

Organizational processes facilitate the accomplishment of desired objectives. As Smith demonstrated, rules and processes in Congress do guide change and influence outcomes (Smith, 1989: 236). Many current operating structures and processes can be adapted to Plenary Review uses. This section will present various devices and procedures which can be used in a Plenary Review format to initiate and support its operation in the U.S. Congress.

The establishment of a separate Plenary Review category for legislative enactments would provide an implementing mechanism. Either two levels of legislative enactment could be created (Plenary Review and statutory) or Plenary Review could be added to current categories as another type (House Resolution, Senate Bill, Continuing Resolution, Plenary Review Resolution, etc.). Not only would such a category give the Plenary Review guiding direction legal standing, it would support the developing recognition of the process.

The fiscal note format might provide a model for a Plenary Review note. Many legislatures have the requirement that a fiscal note be attached to all proposed legislation. The fiscal note simply provides information for legislative consideration of the financial consequences and costs of the proposed legislation. A "Plenary Review note" might require that an assessment of moral, social, economic, political and institutional consequences and a statement of guiding principles be attached to all proposed legislation. This would require that a prior Plenary Review guiding direction be referenced, without foreclosing the opening of further debate as to its application or a change in the guiding direction. Even prior to the adoption of a Plenary Review format, a Plenary Review note would require that proposed legislation consider the arena and its guiding purposes. In this way, Plenary Review perspectives would be added to legislative decisions.

Sunset legislation may also provide a model for Plenary Review. Sunset provisions schedule existing legislative enactments for expiration unless reviewed and approved every seven years. A Plenary Review system will also schedule policy arenas for regular review. If the consequences of present policies are not assessed and guiding purposes reaffirmed (or modified), the legislative enactments in that policy arena would expire every seven to ten years. Such a Plenary Review system would require periodic review and decisions.

The General Accounting Office has developed a concept called "sunrise legislation" (Sundquist, 1981: 340-342). In contrast to sunset legislation, sunrise provisions for review are focused at the beginning rather than at the end. The sunrise notion is to lay the groundwork for oversight in the initial legislation itself. In this approach, the authorizing legislation would include a sunrise section to specify goals, pose oversight questions, and require periodic reports and evaluation. Plenary Review might utilize a similar format by including a section in the authorizing legislation which specifies macro-policy goals and purposes and refers to (or establishes) a guiding direction. In addition, such a section may require periodic stewardship reports, reports of specified consequences, discussion of the relationship to other related policies and programs, and so forth. Even without a full blown Plenary Review system, this approach could stimulate debate which incorporates Plenary Review concerns and could incorporate guiding directions in individual pieces of legislation.

The traditional purpose section of legislation, with all the "whereas" clauses and philosophical statements of goals, can be given more formal meaning and structure in another approach which could be used to implement Plenary Review. In most legislation, this section generally deals with the typical Plenary Review concerns of consequences, required actions and guiding principles. Note, however, the purpose sections of legislative enactments (in the primary mode) do not usually have the level of generality, breath of concern or in-depth evaluation of consequences which Plenary Review is intended to provide. A provision might be adopted to require Plenary Review analysis and guiding direction in the introductory section to all proposed legislation. This would require that each legislative proposal be tied into the policy arena and that macro-policy purposes be considered within which that legislation would fit. This section would refer to the guiding direction and highlight Plenary Review concerns for discussion and debate. Absent a full Plenary Review system, this device could still be used to incorporate Plenary Review perspectives in the consideration of regular legislative actions.

Purpose sections in current legislative enactments are generally ignored in practice (except as legislative history) and they are not given the power of enforcement. Such sections would be more meaningfully drawn were they to be legislative guidelines and binding on executive implementation and judicial interpretation. Susan Rose-Ackerman has presented a paper which raised the concept of making these purpose sections enforceable through judicial action (1988).

She proposed to have courts review the act's statement of purpose and find the statutes unconstitutional if inconsistent with the body of the statute. If the introductory section of legislation tied into a Plenary Review assessment of consequences and guiding direction, this would provide a focus for deliberation and decision. If the Plenary Review section had the status of law, this would provide an enforcement mechanism as courts review the body of the statute and implementing actions for consistency with stated principles.

This section has discussed various devices through which Plenary Review might operate in Congress. At a minimum, Plenary Review concepts and perspectives could be incorporated in current congressional processes. At the maximum, Plenary Review could form a separate second mode complementary to the current format.

INTERACTIVE PLENARY REVIEW WITH THE EXECUTIVE

Plenary Review can go beyond the Congress to include the interaction of the executive and legislative branches, particularly since they both are part of the determination of what public policy in fact is or becomes. Policy proposals and program planning from the executive could initiate congressional review. And in turn, Plenary Review performed in the legislative branch becomes important framework for the implementing decisions, rules and regulations which are the responsibility of the executive branch. An interactive cycle would include: 1) a general Plenary Review assessment of consequences and enactment of guiding directions for a policy arena by the legislature; 2) specific subsequent legislative policy actions within the Plenary Review macro-policy; 3) executive and administrative implementation guided by the statutory provisions and Plenary Review macro-policy guiding direction; 4) regular legislative assessment of consequences and macro-policy adjustments. Each of which are again applied and assessed in further regular iterations. This process inherently includes both the actions and judgements of the legislature and the executive as they share the responsibility of governance.

An interactive Plenary Review system building on existing legislative-executive relationships should provide for substantial executive policy leadership. The President could also initiate the Plenary Review sequence by recommending guiding directions in a policy arena. The President might assign agency review, assemble appropriate information, prepare a stewardship report and assess consequences of programs. At higher administrative levels, the interactions with other programs and agencies, critical junctures, problems and opportunities can be evaluated and options suggested. Such a preparatory Plenary Review would be limited by policy scope and agency perspective, but could form the basis for the review by the political executive and later by the legislature. Based on the preliminary administrative Plenary Review, the chief executive, with the assistance from appropriate staff arms, could conduct a Plenary Review of the policy arena. The President might utilize a Plenary Review unit in the Executive Office of the President, interagency committees of units administering related programs, a cabinet council (utilized in some states) or a super-cabinet (such as proposed by President Nixon) as mechanisms to conduct Plenary Review.

The Plenary Review process in the executive branch would interrelate programs and policy areas. As such, Plenary Review has a major potential for policy development and as a planning mechanism for the President to review general consequences in policy arenas and to propose guiding macro-policy. (In his proposed revision of the Constitution, Rexford Tugwell suggested a similar planning branch to add the long-term view and to prepare general policy proposals; 1970: 52-56.) Plenary Review is a mechanism through which the President can develop and present to Congress a coherent policy program as well as review agency performance. In a real sense, this assessment of consequences, description of goals and guiding directions, and recommendation of appropriate actions would constitute the public policy program of the President on a particular substantive topic. The presidential Plenary Review might then be submitted to Congress along with the stewardship report and supporting information. The information from and the perspective of the chief executive and administrative agencies would all be very useful to Congress in its development of Plenary Review guiding directions.

In this approach, the administrative agencies and the elected executive essentially perform a first-stage Plenary Review. They make their own analysis of performance, gather data, prepare policy rationales, assess consequences and frame proposals for guiding directions for various policy arenas. As submitted to Congress, the general policy of the President for that arena would be considered (much the same way as an executive budget or policy proposal) as the starting point for congressional deliberation, modification and action. As at present, Congress would be constrained only to give full consideration to the submission from the executive branch. Previous analysis simply provides information, expertise, perspective and ideas for congressional deliberation. Congress would then conduct its Plenary Review, as described earlier. After enactment of guiding direction, the congressional Plenary Review would be transmitted back to the President for approval or veto. The regular override provisions would be available to Congress in the case of a presidential veto.

Apart from its contribution to legislative Plenary Review, the use of Plenary Review by the executive can contribute substantially to the needs and functions of the executive branch. Plenary Review serves well both as an administrative review technique and as a strategic thinking approach. Using the established hierarchical groupings of policy assignments for Plenary Review purposes, Plenary Review might be conducted at ascending levels of bureaus, offices and departments. In spite of the disadvantage of grouping by organizational unit rather than policy arena, benefits from the Plenary Review perspective could still be achieved. The Plenary Review perspective of assessing consequences, taking the broad viewer and deliberating guiding principles serves political executives and public managers in their responsibilities.

A Plenary Review Illustration

Science policy may be used to illustrate how Plenary Review will work in congressional review. To establish the context, let it be assumed that Congress has created a special joint Plenary Review Committee to consider science policy. The Committee would include committee and subcommittee members relevant to the topic at hand and other individuals appointed by the leaders of each house. This may be part of a general Plenary Review system where all policy arenas are periodically reviewed, but for the illustration we will posit that Congress is just experimenting with the concept of Plenary Review prior to the establishment of a full process. (Of course, Plenary Review could also be done in each house and its committees).

With the charge to conduct a Plenary Review of science policy, the joint committee would first have to better define the policy arena. They will have to consider the problems and issues which animate this policy arena. They will have to consider such items as basic research, commercialization and the governmental role in supporting research and development. The organizations, programs and policies in the arena would have to be identified. These would range from space and defense to commerce and energy. Judgement will be required to include related and interacting policies and programs, but should not be so broad as to be unmanageable. The definition of the policy arena should take care not just to follow existing policy lines, but should let the issues and problems identify the focus. Such focus would be essential if the deliberation were to reach effective decisions on guiding directions.

Once the policy arena has been described, the Joint Committee will request stewardship reports from the executive branch and charge staff to collect information and data to support deliberations. The stewardship reports would include agency reviews of operations and issues, evaluative data, and recommendations. The stewardship reports will reflect the perspective, experience and preferences of the executive branch, but this rationale is important for Congress to understand in its own review. Presidential recommendations could be requested. As desired, the staff can be assigned to complete special research studies and analysis can be requested from the General Accounting Office, Congressional Research Service and Office of Technology Assessment. Hearings may also be held as determined to be useful. The Joint Committee should supervise the collection of basic information and data.

The critical phase is deliberation ending in decision. The Joint Committee should structure their deliberation to incorporate the elements of Plenary Review. For example, they need to assess the social, moral, economic, political and institutional consequences of past actions in science policy. Where has it brought us? Is this what we intended and want? What prospective consequences do we desire? What is the impact of the federal research and development budget? The broader perspective will compare short term and long range impacts. The wide range of related policies, programs and projects will be reviewed for consistency and interaction. The impacts for defense, private sector business, international competitiveness and technological spin-offs will be considered. Strategies will be debated. The focus on consequences, macro-policy and integration will be difficult to resolve, but the Joint Committee will have to come to some conclusion in a timely way and issue its guiding direction.

The Joint Committee will not have achieved consensus on most items, but it is important to take action and provide leadership in an arena even if the perfect decision is not reached. The decisions will be reached by quantitative vote. What will be decided? The Joint Committee will enact a guiding direction which includes a finding of consequences, an evaluation of priorities (between space and defense, for example), a designation of guiding purposes to be achieved and principles to follow. The guiding direction will be a macro-policy for science policy.

The guiding direction will be referred to both the House and the Senate for their consideration and action. Each house may deliberate, using the information and Joint Committee analysis and guiding direction. Neither house is constrained in any way; each may decide on its own guiding direction. Any difference in outcome would be referred to the Joint Committee (or another conference committee) for reconciliation. As is the current system, each house may approve or return the reconciled version. Once passed by both houses, the guiding direction is established as a formal Plenary Review Resolution (or Congressional Resolution). The guiding direction then has formal status as science macro-policy. All executive implementation and court interpretation in the area would have to refer to the Plenary Review guiding direction. Additional congressional actions would have the macro-policy as a guideline; however, the direction can be changed at any time simply by debating and formally modifying it. Although changes can be made in the guiding direction at any point, the Plenary Review Resolution will provide for automatic review in another seven years.

There are many ways to conduct Plenary Review in the U.S. Congress. This illustration has merely showed one way that Plenary Review might be done.

PLENARY REVIEW AS A FRAMEWORK FOR REFORM

For those interested in constitutional and congressional reform, Plenary Review can be used as a framework for some reforms. This section briefly considers some reform possibilities in the spirit of brainstorming and experimentation. This discussion is speculative; its purpose is to stimulate debate and broaden thinking about possibilities. The four central options which will be considered for Plenary Review are: 1) changing the function of Congress as a whole; 2) differentiating the functions of the two houses; 3) combining the houses for Plenary Review; and 4) adding a Plenary Review body.

Congress as a Plenary Review Body

An argument can be made that Congress should change its function from detailed legislative enactments to the function of Plenary Review. The broader role of system steering and policy coherence are often lost when Congress is enmeshed in the more limited role of detailed policy initiation. Indeed, Congress might be even more influential in a Plenary Review mode in place of the detailed role. In this conception, Congress would assess consequences, evaluate general alternatives and set guiding directions within which specific details would be drawn and implemented through executive and administrative action (which is increasingly the case). Congress in a Plenary Review mode would establish macro-policy and hold the executive branch accountable.

This idea does not appear to be quite so radical when the original Congress and the operation of other legislatures in the world are considered. First, the Constitution never intended Congress to be a "modern organization" characterized by hierarchy, leadership control, division of labor, reliance on written communication and expert staff, and seen as a full-time job and career. Congress might be more usefully conceived of as a deliberative and political body rather than the organizational and hierarchical body it has become. Second, Nelson Polsby has noted that the U.S. Congress is decidedly different from most of the world's legislatures (Shepsle, 1988: 463). In most democratic systems, the legislatures are arenas for debate and general oversight rather than bodies separately initiating detailed policies. Even those based on the Westminster model (including the British Parliament itself) are more deliberative forums and checks on the executive than they are creators of detailed legislation.

In his review of Congress for the American Assembly, Samuel Huntington has also suggested redefining the function of Congress (1965: 29-31). Rather than fighting current forces, Huntington has suggested intensifying and incorporating these forces in a revised congressional function. "Congress is in a dilemma," he maintained, "because opinion conceives of it as a legislature." If it gave up the effort to be a legislature, he wrote, it might play a "much more positive and influential role in our political system as a whole." He noted that "representative assemblies have not always been legislatures." In this conception, Congress would perform a review and legitimizing function, rather than initiating detailed legislation. In most countries around the world (he cited a survey of forty-one nations), parliaments and representative assemblies are losing power in initiation and legislation while gaining power in the control of government activity. In fact, Congress is unusual; it is the exception. Huntington has argued that it is more important to preserve the Congress as a governing control than as an initiator of detailed legislation. This is an intensification, rather than reversal of direction, he maintained, because it would legitimize and expand the current trends toward constituent service, legislative oversight and check and balance.

More recently, Mezey has argued that "the United States will not have a government capable of achieving good public policy until the American people change the way in which they think about government and based on that rethinking, make changes in their political institutions" (Mezey, 1989: xiii-xiv). In specific, he has maintained that the expectations concerning the role of Congress should shift from those that emphasize its role as an initiator and designer of public policy to those that emphasize its role as a representative body. In his view, the Congress as a representational legislature would not design detailed public policy, but would continue to affect it. Congress would engage in open debate on issues of the day. He used the metaphor of a lens to describe its function of reflecting and intensifying public opinion on policy issues, oversee the executive, establish boundaries, and determine the public interest.

> Thus, a Congress organized in accord with the representational model would not be viewed as the incubator and designer of public policy—something that it does poorly—but instead as a body that would publicly discuss policy problems and potential solutions, aggressively oversee the executive as it develops and implements public policy, continuously hold the executive to account for its actions, and through its members, represent to the executive the needs of individual constituents, the interests of the constituency as a whole, and collectively, the opinions of the nation at large. A Congress so conceived would be doing what legislatures do well—ensuring the democratic nature of the public policy process. (Mezey, 1989: 200-202)

Applied to Plenary Review, the notions of Huntington and Mezey suggest that the Congress of the United States approve legislation, deliberate policy consequences, establish broad guidelines, evaluate directions and principles, check and balance, and perform oversight of outcomes. It is argued that Congress would be more effective in a

Plenary Review role operating at a more general level than as an initiator of detailed legislation. Congress may have even greater control through determining macro-policy, assessing the consequences of that policy and its detailed micro-policies, and making guiding adjustments.

This conception of a revised congressional role is very useful for the consideration of Plenary Review. First, it provides the courage to think along lines other than the current model and it suggests other important functions which might be performed. Second, it helps to conceptualize reform as an intensification and culmination of, rather than reversal of, trends. Third, this revision of the function of the United States Congress suggests answers to some of the important questions posed to Plenary Review. For example, the difficult question about where Congress would find the time and energy to accomplish Plenary Review is answered in large part by replacing the current assignment with a more important general one.

A Different Role for the Senate

Each house of Congress does not need to duplicate exactly the function of the other to have a working check and balance system. In another possible adaptation, the Senate might be assigned a Plenary Review function while the House could continue the current legislative function. The minor differences in chamber responsibilities (money bills originating in the House, advice and consent in the Senate, Senate approval of treaties, etc.) would be made more extreme. The House might pass regular legislation and the Senate might simply review rather than initiate legislation, repeat hearings and so forth. The arrangement might be similar to the review the House of Lords gives to enactments of the House of Commons.

Taking the notion a bit further, the Senate might establish the general sense of policy, the guiding directions, and the House would then act within these developing directions in an iterative fashion with the Senate. In this concept, the Senate would become a deliberative, guiding, philosophical, reflective and broad view body—a Plenary Review body. The House of Representatives would then act within the framework set by the Senate. With the House developing detailed legislative enactments and the Senate approving or disapproving, the bicameral check and balance would continue.

In his proposal for a revised constitution, Rexford Tugwell has suggested a similar change in function for the Senate (1976: 61-71, 119-121, 175-176). His intent was to make the Senate more of a national body, one with a national rather than a parochial perspective. In his proposed constitution, the Senate is made a "general considering body" by revising its membership to include former presidents and vice presidents, past court justices (he suggested court reforms as well), former heads of republics (groupings of states), unsuccessful candidates for president and vice president, leading citizens, outstanding retired civil officers and others. His Senate would take the broad view, give general guidance, and debate general values and directions from a national perspective.

Combined Houses for Plenary Review

Another possible arrangement for Plenary Review in Congress is to maintain the current operation as it now exists, but to combine the two chambers periodically in a new and separate mode for Plenary Review. This would maintain the current bicameral relationship while creating a joint (unicameral) arrangement for Plenary Review purposes.

A similar sort of arrangement can be found in the Norwegian *Storting* and the Icelandic *Althingi* where there are two separate bodies but where some functions are performed in a unicameral arrangement (Andren, 1964: 102-104). In the *Althingi*, for example, the bicameral chambers deal with regular legislative matters which can be introduced in either chamber. At the same time, the two chambers combine into a unicameral format to deal with finance and budget matters, assisted by a joint Committee on Finance representing the combined parliament. The finance bill is never submitted to the separate divisions; it is a matter for the unicameral arrangement alone. In essence, the parliament is both bicameral and unicameral (tricameral?) in that some functions are handled in the two body format and other functions are handled in the joint arrangement.

In some ways, Congress already has a third legislative body in the conference committees where key decisions are made in reconciling actions of the House and Senate. Royce Hanson and his colleagues at the Humphrey Institute of Public Affairs (University of Minnesota) have noted this same issue in their analysis of the Minnesota Legislature (Hanson, 1989). They recommend a unicameral legislature to make the legislative process more deliberative and accountable.

Adapted to Plenary Review, the U.S. Congress could function in the bicameral format for current legislative responsibilities. It could then combine periodically for the Plenary Review function. This would be a separate arrangement with a different focus and function—the broad overview, macro-policy, system direction and general guiding purposes.

Adding a Plenary Review Body

Another approach would maintain the current Congress, but add another higher body to accomplish Plenary Review. This notion is similar to proposals made by various scholars.

Frederick Hayek argued for a body above Congress, a super-congress (1978: 99-103). In his view, such a body would provide a needed function which is not now performed. While Congress directs current government activities, a super-congress would have the power to articulate "general rules of just conduct." One focuses on the operations of government; the other focuses on what is right. One operates naturally on the competition of interests; the other is intended, to use his term, to be a "senate of the wise." Hayek argued that one body can not perform well both functions. The interests and politics of a body dealing with specific programs and legislative actions is not conducive to laying down rules of just conduct. He anticipated that lobbying and interest orientation would not pressure an assembly confined to the "articulation of universally applicable rules of just conduct, whose effects on particular individuals or groups would be unforeseeable" (Hayek, 1978: 100). The notion which Hayek proposed has some relationship to the Plenary Review function. The super-congress would assess general consequences and determine guiding directives.

More recently, Donald Robinson has proposed a federal council of one hundred notables. The council would be appointed for life by the President with the advice of Congress. The overall purpose is to obtain "coherent action and responsibility" (Robinson, 1987). Bernard Baruch suggested a "supreme court of business" to deliberate actions, policies and principles in order to respond to the challenges of the Great Depression (Baruch, 1930). He intended the group to be a deliberative and thinking, rather than regulatory, body. The disparate concerns of Tugwell, Hayek, Baruch and Robinson all illustrate the need to have a body focus on macro-policies and general principles. That is, there is an important need for the Plenary Review function to be performed.

Another variant of this idea is Plenary Review select commissions created and charged by Congress to review a policy arena. Commissions could be created for major policy arenas on a regular cycle. Each commission may have a life cycle of three years; perhaps two years to collect information and perform studies and one year for deliberation and decision. The select commission might be composed of appointees from the President and majority and minority leaders in Congress. Commission members could include members of Congress, major public figures, experts and representatives of differing views—such as was included in the Commission which dealt with Social Security financing. A select commission would be like a super-congress except that there would be different commissions for different policy arenas. The guiding direction issuing from a select commission could be handled in different ways. It could be automatically adopted unless rejected by a super-majority in Congress (say 2/3 or 3/4); it could be submitted to Congress as a recommendation; or it could be used by Congress to develop information, define issues and set the stage for a congressional Plenary Review.

SUMMARY

This chapter has applied Plenary Review to the United States Congress. The discussion first illustrated how Plenary Review might operate in the current congressional system. It suggested how Congress can review policy consequences and effectively steer the American polity. The main notions can be summarized in the following points.

- Plenary Review can generally be conducted within the current structure and procedures of Congress.
  - Congress can operate Plenary Review as a supplementary and separate mode in which they would assess consequences and establish guiding purposes.
  - Plenary Review would provide a process and perspective which would make Congress more effective.
- Alternative arrangements which might be used for Plenary Review are:
  - Plenary Review can be conducted on the floor of the House and Senate.

- Plenary Review may be done by the committees and subcommittees in their areas of assignment.
- Special joint or Plenary Review committees can be established.
- Implementing devices which may be used to facilitate Plenary Review in Congress include the use of existing procedures, Plenary Review note, sunset legislation, sunrise legislation, and purpose sections of legislation.
- Plenary Review can be usefully conducted as a joint interactive process between the legislature and executive.
  - Plenary Review in the executive branch can provide the foundation for legislative Plenary Review.
  - Plenary Review can serve the executive and administrative agencies as an administrative review technique and as a policy development and strategic thinking approach.

Second, the Chapter presented Plenary Review as a reform framework to deal with some of these concerns for constitutional and congressional effectiveness. Four main possibilities were developed.

- First, Congress may be more effective performing the general Plenary Review functions of assessing consequences and determining macro-policy than the role of enacting detailed legislation.
- Second, the Senate could perform the Plenary Review function while the House of Representatives continues to focus on detailed legislation.
- Third, another option would be to continue the current bicameral arrangement, but add a separate joint arrangement for Plenary Review.
- Fourth, Plenary Review might be accomplished in a separate body—a super-congress, a council of elders or a select commission.

Ten:
Adoption of Plenary Review in Policy Bodies

Change is a major challenge, particularly in a governmental system known for its intractability. What would be required for Plenary Review to be adopted in various policy bodies at various levels? How might Plenary Review be effectively established to contribute to the making of public policy? Since Plenary Review will be a challenging change in most contexts, this chapter will discuss forces influencing adoption and possible strategies for change.

There are no easy keys to effective change, but the American system might be able to accommodate some political changes. In *Political Innovations in America*, Nelson Polsby argued that policy innovations generally follow the state of tension caused by need and an idea or notion responding to that need (1984: xii, 18). Two requisite factors for adopting innovation, Polsby contended, are first, an underlying cultural disposition favoring the application of rational thought to problems, and second, incentives in the political system to search for innovations. His conclusion is that "both these conditions are clearly met in the American political system" (1984: 165). As the need is increasingly recognized and as Plenary Review can be shown to contribute to that need, these underlying conditions warrant a hopeful optimism that Plenary Review may be adopted.

While Plenary Review may be more easily established in some applications such as city councils, legislative committees and task forces, adoption in many other applications will face serious obstacles. Adoption for congressional use is a particularly daunting challenge. Patterson has contended that a marked transformation of Congress "simply has not occurred in the whiggish context of American political history," (1978: 133). But innovations must originate somewhere and there is change over time. Without discounting the challenges, a hopeful optimism encourages the Plenary Review attempt to improve policy making. Lord Bryce, in his well-known study of the American political system, wrote: "A hundred times in writing this book have I been disheartened by the facts I was stating; A hundred times has the recollection of the abounding strength and vitality of the nation chased away these tremors" (Keller, 1988: 92). Those who have developed Plenary Review argue that the American political system may be capable of more than frequently thought and that we should dedicate effort to innovations which can stimulate improvement. With the recognition of the challenge and an optimistic hope, the issues of development and adoption will be considered.

PLENARY REVIEW AS A DEVELOPMENTAL PROCESS

Most change occurs in a developmental process. First, all policy bodies change and adapt; the only questions are how much, why and in what directions. It is not a matter of change; it is a matter of changing in directions more beneficial and at rates more effective. The Plenary Review concept can guide the change which will naturally occur. Second, the nature of Plenary Review may make development easier. Transplantation into the body politic of a rigidly prescribed reform proposal would be more difficult than establishment of a concept such as Plenary Review which is intended to be adaptive. Third, public policy bodies are often reformed as members and sub-units gradually incorporate better ideas and procedures. Using Congress as an example, the initial acceptance of Plenary Review may not be more than one sub-committee on retreat, a staff report assessing consequences and integrating policy arenas, or the interest of one member of Congress. Fourth, there will be many decision points for use of Plenary Review concepts (not just one watershed decision). Initial experiences will likely grow and expand as the concept proves useful.

As applications expand, Plenary Review will itself influence further development. That is, Plenary Review will likely be an incubated innovation (to use Polsby's term, 1984: 158). Adoption will be gained through research, learning by doing, further conceptual development and experimental application. A challenging concept, such as Plenary Review, particularly requires this approach. It will be necessary to stumble, adapt, muddle through, grope, and patiently pursue. In the beginning stages of a developmental process, concern will be largely with the need, risks, hopes and desires, and confirming and disconfirming experience. There will be uncertain phases requiring intuitive experimentation and creative insight in adapting to the need. Learning and reframing ultimately lead to full application and effective response (see Quinn, 1988: 17).

This book has presented Plenary Review as a concept. The concept, of course, is a mere first step. The Plenary Review notion will have to be translated from the conceptual and abstract to the specific and applied. The development of a general system with its attendant procedures and rules will require experience and time. It will be necessary to develop specialized structures and processes. This is one reason Plenary Review has been approached as a developmental process reflecting core elements rather than as a rigid technique to be plugged into all situations. The specific systems and processes can develop within each separate context utilizing the rules and norms of each policy body. Although Plenary Review can utilize many existing procedures and mechanisms, some adaptation and will be necessary.

In its prime application to the United States Congress, Plenary Review provides a developmental model for change efforts. The absence of an adequate guiding model of what Congress is or could be has contributed to the lack of effective change and a preference for the status quo. Where there is no overall conception, reform efforts have no guide or criteria (Davidson, 1966: 2-3). Since there is no one accepted model of what a legislature ought to be (Huitt, 1965: 99), there are disagreements on the premises, the route and the goal. Plenary Review will be useful as a developmental model and vision of the congressional role in policy making.

Even with Plenary Review as a model, the complexity of factors in its adoption will require recognition and evaluation of trade-offs in each policy body. Debates over congressional reform, for example, have long stalled on these trade-offs. Opposite choices can both have merit. For example, an efficient and prompt legislature may hinder an open and deliberative process (Rieselbach, 1977: 68-88). Otherwise beneficial changes in legislative leadership and streamlining of congressional procedures may reduce the democratic nature of the legislature. To deal with these matters is to deal with grand debates, such as trade-offs between leadership versus democratic control, specialization versus generalization, rationalist expert knowledge versus generalist political knowledge, written communication versus face-to-face interaction, and professional position versus citizen duty. One can not choose between these options solely on empirical grounds; the judgements have to be normative, speculative and tentative. And, when change is attempted, there is no insurance that it will always accomplish the desired outcome or even that it will move toward the ends sought. In his discussion of constitutional reform, James Sundquist noted that structures which enable the government to move decisively to do good things will also enable it to move with dispatch to do bad things (1986: 12). At the same time, however, these complexities do not warrant inaction. Plenary Review provides an adaptive process to guide effective change in the Congress of the United States and other public policy bodies.

FORCES FOR PLENARY REVIEW ESTABLISHMENT

While there are no easy steps to the adoption of any concept, there are key forces which can lead to more effective establishment. The forces of external influences, political processes, network of champions, internal incentives and formative processes will be discussed in the following sections as they might be used for the adoption of Plenary Review.

External Influences for Change

Forces outside the various public policy bodies work for change. As contexts change and as policy demands grow, policy bodies are forced to consider better ways of doing things. As developing challenges render policy responses unacceptable and as crises require the broader view, Plenary Review can help policy bodies to be more effective and responsive. Thus, external events and needs may force the consideration of Plenary Review and other innovations. Turbulent times, constituency group pressures, commanding ideas, legislative-executive competition and policy failures can heighten pressures for better policy performance. Crises may surface in specific policy areas, such as environment, banking, international relations, energy or poverty. Linden has written that most change is "pain-driven," that change comes from the felt need for that change (Linden, 1990: 42-46).

While innovations may be induced by crisis or catastrophe, action in many public policy arenas might best be taken in anticipation before the turbulence of crisis. It may not be wise to wait for crisis to force change—or to wait for calmer times, for that matter. Although some would argue for unplanned incremental change, evolving and never moving faster than acceptance and experience allow, such change may be inadequate to meet the contending needs and changing policy circumstances. There are occasions when grander steps are required and when leadership must anticipate the future not merely hold to the past. Plenary Review calls for effort now to develop adequate and periodic response to developing public policy needs, for assessment of public macro-policy and for governance action as required.

Outside forces may be particularly important for congressional adoption of Plenary Review. Because the political agenda in Congress always has many separate matters clamoring for attention, it may well take an outside stimulus to get Congress to consider a major change (Sinclair, 1985: 312-313). At the same time, Congress is a democratically responsive and representative organization which necessarily reacts to external forces. Charles Jones has observed that Congress is not a "self-starting" institution; therefore, "creating a climate of support for change among the general public *outside* Congress may overcome the resistance to change inherent in existing processes and structures" (1975: 273-275). Sinclair also concluded that significant changes can usually be traced to a change in the broader, politically relevant environment and "such change is not generated within the Congress" (1985: 312-313). Present challenges and external forces increasingly make effective response in Congress more necessary—and likely.

The development of Plenary Review in a policy body will be greatly influenced by the context of that body. There are complex factors in each environment which both support and limit change. There are always a variety of contending forces at work within a representative democracy. For example, diversity and fragmentation increase the likelihood that innovations will be conceived and proposed, but decrease the likelihood that they can be easily adopted (Wilson, 1966: 200). Even a good-faith effort can not always determine or control the outcome because it will be influenced and modified by the environmental context.

TABLE 10-1
FORCE FOR ADOPTION: EXTERNAL INFLUENCES

Actions which support the adoption of Plenary Review include:

- Develop Plenary Review in response to crises and needs
- Respond to external forces using Plenary Review to meet concerns
- Improve external support through internal improvements
- Demonstrate how Plenary Review can improve institutional and policy shortcomings
- Avert crises and problems through anticipatory use
- Build support in constituencies external to the policy body

Support Through Political Processes

The development and adoption of an innovation may be seen essentially as a political process (Wilson, 1966: 203). The establishment of a new notion usually occurs through the political process rather than as a simple planned implementation (Stone, 1985: 484). Thus, political skill and acumen become critical to acceptance and institutionalization (Garner, 1988: 2). In the congressional development of Plenary Review, for example, the political nature of the process makes critical the ability to identify supporters, build coalitions, balance interests and create networks. And because Congress is a body which is diverse and fragmented, it will be more difficult to reach a decision and more bargaining will be required.

In *From Vision to Reality*, Linden has studied the approaches used by successful government innovators (Linden, 1990: 7). He has noted the need to adapt and respond to political forces. In the U.S. Congress, for example, "the perfect is the enemy of the good." The perfect bill does not survive intact. Innovations must give and take, compromise to form coalitions, maintain flexibility, keep a generalist approach and continue the process of innovation and adaptation.

The political process operates largely through informal action rather than administrative directive. Formal institutional imposition can mean little if the underlying support and acceptance do not exist.

As Don Price points out, fundamental problems can not be met by legalistic language alone (such as in the formal Constitution) but only by political consensus and political change in the unwritten constitution of practice and acceptance (1983: 14). The political process of garnering support will be necessary to create a foundation for successful development of Plenary Review.

TABLE 10-2
FORCE FOR ADOPTION:
DEVELOPMENT OF POLITICAL SUPPORT

Actions which support the adoption of Plenary Review include:

- Build coalitions and develop networks
- Build understanding of the concept as prelude to acceptance
- Provide leadership and establish linkages with other leaders
- Meet mutual needs in the use of Plenary Review
- Develop informal organizational and political relationships
- Anticipate and adapt to roadblocks by working with affected parties
- Demonstrate how Plenary Review can work and can meet mutual needs

Network of Champions

Successful change often depends on a network of champions (Garner, 1988: 4-9). Even good ideas can languish without champions who believe in the change or zealots who push to fruition. Champions muster the initial energy to create and direct the developmental process. The larger and more complex the situation, the stronger the need for a network of champions. A network of champions for Plenary Review might include proponents in the legislature, executive, administrative agencies, advocacy organizations, think tanks, constituent groups and influential citizens.

Les Garner has argued that effective champions are more dependent on a thorough understanding of the need for change than on a program plan. He has maintained that "getting the idea off the ground requires, more than anything else, a creator, the individual who takes the idea and is willing to try it and stake his legitimacy on its success. This single champion can give the idea shape and gain the necessary approval for the idea to get a trial" (Garner, 1988: 10). For Plenary Review, the challenge currently is to develop, nurture and present the notion of Plenary Review. Later, it will be important to add implementing champions, those with access and influence in the arena of practice. Its appeal and utility should help develop the necessary support. Champions—change agents who understand and believe and who work diligently to shepherd the idea—will be critical to the adoption of Plenary Review.

TABLE 10-3
FORCE FOR ADOPTION:
NETWORK OF CHAMPIONS

Actions which support the adoption of Plenary Review include:

- Build an enabling network of supporters
- Present Plenary Review to broader audiences
- Expand experience with Plenary Review in wider group
- Involve organizations and people in Plenary Review experiments
- Publicize the concept in various forums and media
- Continue to adapt the concept in broader discussions and applications

The art of building a network is the art of developing concepts for change that satisfy some enduring need and appeal to others on their own terms (Garner, 1988: 6). A growing network of champions for Plenary Review will develop as its advantages for a policy body, its members and its constituents are recognized. Drucker maintained that innovation is both conceptual and perceptual (Drucker, 1985: 134-139). Many problems are embedded in our thinking and perceiving (Morgan, 1986: 335). Crossing conceptual barriers can be key to development. Establishing a clear perspective of the Plenary Review concept can be the prelude to adoption. The force of an idea is important in building networks. A sound concept, effectively presented, can provide a guiding force and motivation. Without a sound concept, the effort flounders; without understanding, acceptance is usually lacking; without belief, implementation is difficult. Plenary Review is still at the stage of developing the concept and learning to present it effectively; the other challenges lie ahead. Development of Plenary Review will be greatly dependent on establishing an effective understanding and perspective of the concept in the governance system it addresses. It is not sufficient for only the architects of change to "understand" the system and the need; this same vision must be powerful enough to attract the support of others.

Internal Incentives for Change

Internal incentives are important not only for initial development but for effective operation as well. Put simply, what would make it in the interest of a policy body—such as Congress—to do Plenary Review? What is keeping the body from doing Plenary Review now? What are the internal incentives for change? What internal forces limit change?

The internal forces in a policy body exist in a vigorous mix of interactions, rewards, interests, costs, politics, operations and processes. In Congress, for example, committee routines, agency contacts, interest group relationships, power and career interests can easily induce the member of Congress to ignore the broad view and spend little time assessing past and prospective consequences in an orderly way. As Burns has maintained, "even if machinery were changed, the pattern of political motivations, perceptions, ambitions, rewards, deprivations, and other behaviors surrounding that machinery could not so easily be transformed" (1984: 188). Any change, such as Plenary Review, will have to work within these internal incentives to be effective.

To be fully successful, any change must benefit the policy body itself as well as its members. For example, Congress must be convinced initially and then find and receive continuing incentives that a change, such as Plenary Review, is in the general interest and in their specific interest. A change in the system can not effectively arise solely from the rationale of the notion. Wilson has contended that changes proposed from outside an organization lead to innovation only as these changes modify present or prospective incentives (1966: 210). A longtime Congressional scholar, Richard Fenno, noted that "it is the members who run Congress" and that we get "pretty much the kind of Congress that they want" (1975: 287). So, the development of an effective Plenary Review system is dependent in great part on meeting current incentives or creating different incentives (or, less likely, creating different kinds of members of Congress and other policy bodies).

Table 10-4 identifies some general incentives for individual legislators. It also notes how Plenary Review can meet some of these legislative motivations.

TABLE 10–4
PLENARY REVIEW AND LEGISLATIVE INCENTIVES

General Legislative Incentives:

- Improved public policy effectiveness
- Re-election
- Power within the Legislature
- External power
- Personal reputation and gain

Plenary Review Can Meet Some Legislative Incentives Through:

- Greater impact on policy outcomes
- Increased reputation from policy stands and actions
- Improved public policy and public view of the legislature
- Ability to assess and adapt policy to desired consequences
- Greater power in deliberation and decision
- Increased impact relative to the other branches

Taking Congress as a prime application and illustration for Plenary Review, there are some internal incentives in Congress for adoption of Plenary Review. In a successful Plenary Review system, members of Congress could take and defend positions which add to their reputation, recognition, power, credit and electoral advantage. Congressional power thereby might increase in relation to the executive. Increasing the effectiveness of public policies themselves can be an important incentive. Power, often regarded as a basic motivation of the members of Congress (Dodd, 1985: 490-491), might increase in various ways from Plenary Review.

TABLE 10-5
FORCE FOR ADOPTION:
INTERNAL INCENTIVES

Actions which support the adoption of Plenary Review include:

- Recognize existing power relationships in applications
- Illustrate how Plenary Review will enable more effective public policy
- Develop through experience how Plenary Review can increase recognition and role
- Illustrate how policy body members can receive credit for body effectiveness
- Show that Plenary Review can provide more insight and control in directing policies and the polity
- Identify those who would increase influence and power in Plenary Review

Of course, there are other and opposite incentives. Reluctance to modify established power relationships in congressional assignments, structures and processes will limit change. The potential difficulties of disturbing internal politics and operations and the uncertainties about a new distribution of power in Plenary Review are well illustrated by the problems in the related area of congressional oversight. Dodd has concluded that Congress fails to conduct effective oversight *not* because there are no incentives (such as power) and *not* because it is not to electoral advantage (such as leadership and publicity). Congress fails to conduct oversight, Dodd maintained, because "most members of Congress *fear* its impact on the authority of their existing committee assignments and *fear* the power that a strong oversight committee would have in Congress and in national policy making" (1985: 510-511). Dodd also commented that attempts since the 1970s to deal with congressional problems of leadership, coordination, accountability, insulation and oversight have been crippled by this preoccupation for personal power. While any attempt at Plenary Review would realistically face these same problems, there are also the potential advantages of policy leadership, personal recognition and political power. And, of course, the emergence of policy effectiveness in dealing with the broad perspective and providing future guidance for governance are important incentives.

The Impact of a Formative Structure and Process

People and internal incentives influence development; however, a process also exerts an influence on people and the internal incentives. That is, a Plenary Review system, over time, could itself help create the experience and incentives required for its eventual success. Such a process or system in most policy bodies has no formal barriers. For example, the founders gave the national legislature considerable freedom to organize itself as it saw fit. Aside from the formal specification of a presiding officer in each chamber, the Constitution allowed Congress to select its own organization and process (Shepsle, 1988: 464-465). The process of Plenary Review—clearly within the bounds of operation which Congress may prescribe for itself—can provide a formative influence which will enable its further development.

Davidson, Kovenock and O'Leary have compared two competing approaches to congressional change: rational problem solving and incrementalism (1966: 5-6). The rationalists state their case in the long-range and propose comprehensive developments. The pragmatic incrementalists tend to cast their analysis and proposals in terms of current political feasibility. The rational approach often fails to consider how to move from today to what is intended for tomorrow; the incremental approach often leads to an intellectual dead-end because what is needed may not come from the particular problems and may be based primarily on political feasibility. With the limitations inherent in each approach, they have called for a new strategy of "incremental idealism" which combines a vision of the future with practical techniques for change. Plenary Review suggests a step which goes even further: an adaptive process which continues to evaluate and evolve as the institution is transformed and as contextual challenges change.

Linden evaluated various approaches used by government innovators to implement management innovations (Linden, 1990: 42-46). He found that structural changes can lead to other changes. He noted that change does not have to begin with an attitudinal shift. If a change is made in structure or process, attitudinal changes may follow.

An initial Plenary Review process may enable a transformation into a well operating system; as the process guides operation, new values are created and experience grows. If a Plenary Review process is able to engage some participants then additional supporting acceptance and incentives may follow. Transformation in a Plenary Review system will be a complex, interdependent and interactive process—a chicken and egg challenge. Process breeds acceptance, but acceptance is necessary to effectively develop the process. Establishment of an initial process could be the first step to full and effective operation and acceptance.

The establishment of an initial Plenary Review process is also an important step in building capacity. The development of information, skills, support units, procedures, communication networks, exemplary projects, processes and standards will occur through experience and trial. This iterative process of experience and development may occur more easily in some applications than others, but a developmental process will be necessary as each policy body implements Plenary Review.

The simplest transforming process is a phase-in period, of both developing process and experience step by step. Much as a child develops by understanding a concept, by willingness to try and by experience, Plenary Review will require a phase-in. Using the Congress as an illustration, Plenary Review can start in a few trials in the development of suitable policy arenas, the establishment of Plenary Review schedules and procedures, and then initiation of the review cycle, which itself may cover as many as ten years. In effect, as many as a dozen years would be required for establishment and completion of the first cycle. (See US House, Rules Committee, 1980, for the extensive operations required to implement a proposed comprehensive sunset review system.)

There are benefits to a gradual adoption of Plenary Review. As a concept, Plenary Review requires both development and experimentation; it requires adaptation to the needs and norms of the individual policy bodies. And, in terms of strategy, it is often more effective to prepare the groundwork and take limited actions which move in the desired direction than to attempt adoption of a comprehensive reform proposal (Jones, 1975: 273). Since Congress and other policy bodies are always changing anyway, small changes may be more easily incorporated in this process than major changes (Ripley, 1983: 408: Dodd, 1985: 489).

TABLE 10-6
FORCE FOR ADOPTION:
TRANSFORMATIVE STRUCTURE

Actions which support the adoption of Plenary Review include:

- Create experimental elements of Plenary Review as a start
- Build on experience to adapt and develop Plenary Review
- Establish the structures and processes necessary for Plenary Review
- Experiment with limited applications to develop understanding and experience

The developmental path for Plenary Review, and other like innovations, will lead from conception to experimentation to implementation. Most change is difficult; significant change is often very difficult. The body politic often finds it difficult to accept a new organ transplant, even when it is to its own benefit. The formal adoption of Plenary Review in Congress and other legislative bodies will likely be dependent on: 1) political and organizational support; 2) external influences for change, particularly crises; 3) development of champions and the building of an enabling network; 4) internal incentives, including member benefit and institutional effectiveness; and 5) creation of a transformative structure and process which will allow Plenary Review to grow gradually through the refinement of experience.

STRATEGIES FOR DIFFERENT CONTIGENCIES

Strategies will need to be different for different purposes, in different applications and at different points. Two important factors in determining the appropriate strategy are, first, the degree of understanding and acceptance of the Plenary Review concept, and second, the adaptive capacity of the policy body—such as Congress—to adopt and operate Plenary Review. Each of these may range from strong to weak. When combined, they suggest different strategies for different situations.

TABLE 10-7
STATEGIES FOR PLENARY REVIEW ADOPTION

	Conceptual Development and Acceptance of Plenary Review	
Adaptive Capacity of Policy Body	Weak	Strong
Weak	**I** • Muddling Through • Innovation • Concept Development • Concept Deliberation	**II** • Experimentation • Program Development • Step by Step Approach • Capacity Building
Strong	**III** • Pilot Programs • Experiential Development • Development of Support • Education	**IV** • Bold Initiatives • Full Adoption • Implementation • Timely Action

The matrix describes different strategies for different situations. When the concept is well developed and accepted and when the adaptive capacity of the policy body is strong (quadrant IV), then is the time for bold initiatives, timely action and implementation. If the concept is still fuzzy, support is questionable and adaptive capacity is weak (quadrant I), the most appropriate approach will be innovative development of the concept and discussion centered on possible applications. When the concept and its acceptance are uncertain, but the adaptive capacity is strong (quadrant III), the time is right for pilot programs, learning through doing, developing acceptance and educating for understanding. The last case is when there is weak adaptive capacity but strong understanding and acceptance of Plenary

Review (quadrant II); in this situation experimentation, capacity building and a step-by-step approach are appropriate.

The current general situation is one with a good concept but weak adaptive capacity in most policy bodies (moving from quadrant I to II). This suggests that experience and missionary work are appropriate in working for adoption of Plenary Review. Experience will demonstrate benefits, build capacity and further develop the concept. Missionary work will spread the concept, encourage use and stimulate thinking about such improvements.

In *Innovation and Entrepreneurship*, Peter Drucker provided suggestions for successful changes (Drucker, 1985: 134-139). Purposeful, systematic innovation begins with an analysis of the opportunities and needs. Innovation is both conceptual and perceptual. To be effective, he noted, innovation should be simple and focused and should start small. And, successful innovation aims at leadership. The Plenary Review project has attempted to respond to a critical need, and to be both conceptual and innovative. Thus far, it has attempted to be relatively simple and to experiment in smaller settings. The challenge is now to present the concept to a wider audience, particularly those in leadership capacities in the public sector. As the initial efforts develop, further steps and strategies become possible.

SUMMARY

This chapter has discussed the adoption of Plenary Review. The establishment and effective operation of Plenary Review will be influenced the following factors.

- Plenary Review is best established as a developmental process rather than a rigid technique.
  - Plenary Review will fit the current processes of most policy bodies.
  - At the same time, it will need to be adapted to the context and needs of each body.
- The establishment of Plenary Review will be dependent on the following forces:
  - Acceptance and support through the political process,
  - External influences for change, particularly crises and policy demands,

Adoption in Policy Bodies

- Champions and supporters in an enabling network,
- Internal incentives, including member benefit and institutional effectiveness, and
- A formative, initial Plenary Review structure and process which will allow it to grow gradually through experience and accomplishment.

- The strategies for development of Plenary Review will vary according to the acceptance of the concept and the adaptive capacity of the policy body to operate Plenary Review. These two factors suggest the following strategies for establishment:
  - Conceptual development, research and discussion,
  - Experimentation, program development and capacity building,
  - Pilot programs, experiential development, development of support, and education, and
  - Finally, bold initiatives, adoption and implementation.

BIBLIOGRAPHY

Abelson, Philip H. 1988. "Competitiveness: A Long-Enduring Problem." *Science* 240 (May): 65.

Ackoff, Russell L. 1974. *Redesigning the Future: A Systems Approach to Societal Problems.* New York, NY: John Wiley.

American Assembly. 1965. *The Congress and America's Future* David Truman, editor. Englewood Cliffs, NJ: Prentice-Hall.

Anderson, Annelise and Dennis L. Bark, editors. 1988. *Thinking About America: The United States in the 1990s.* Stanford, CA: Hoover Institute.

Andren, Nils. 1964. *Government and Politics in the Nordic Countries: Denmark, Finland, Iceland, Norway, Sweeden.* Stockholm: Almqvist and Wiksell.

Argyris, Chris. 1982. *Reasoning, Learning and Action.* San Francisco, CA: Jossey Bass.

____ and D.A. Schon. 1978. *Organizational Learning: A Theory of Action Perspective.* Reading, MA: Addison-Wesley.

Asher, Herbert B. and Herbert F. Weisberg. 1985. "Voting Change in Congress: Some Dynamic Perspectives on an Evolutionary Process," *Studies of Congress.* Glenn R. Parker, editor. Washington, D.C.: Congressional Quarterly Press: 420-446.

Bach, Stanley and Steven S. Smith. 1988. *Managing Uncertainty in the House of Representatives: Adaptation and Innovation in Special Rules.* Washington, DC: The Brookings Institution.

Barber, Benjamin R. 1979. "The Compromised Republic: Public Purposelessness in America." *The Moral Foundations of the American Republic.* Charlottesville, VA: University Press of Virginia: 19-38. Baruch, Barnard M. "Baruch Proposes 'Court of Business.'" *New York Times* (April 30, 1930).

Bardach, Eugene. 1977. *The Implementation Game: What Happens After a Bill Becomes a Law?* Cambridge, MA: MIT Press.

Benjamin, Roger and Stephen L. Elkin, editors. 1985. *The Democratic State.* Lawrence, Kansas: University Press of Kansas.

Bennis, Warren. 1989. *Why Leaders Can't Lead: The Unconscious Conspiracy Continues.* San Francisco, CA: Jossey-Bass.

Benveniste, Guy. 1989. *Mastering the Politics of Planning.* San Francisco, CA: Jossey-Bass.

Bolling, Richard. 1965. *House Out of Order.* New York, NY: Dutton.

Boren, David L. 1991. "Major Repairs for Congress," *Washington Post,* August 6, 1991: A15.

Brenner, Philip. 1983. *The Limits and Possibilities of Congress.* New York, NY: St. Martin's Press.

Broder, David. 1991. "Congress Dealt With Gravity of Subject," *Dominion Post,* January 16, 1991.

Brodkin, Evelyn Z. 1987. "Party Politics: If We Can't Govern, Can We Manage?" *Political Science Quarterly* 102: (Winter) 571-587.

Brookings. 1987. "Restoring Effective Government: A Conversation on Constitutional Reform with Lloyd N. Cutler, James L. Sundquist, and Paul E. Peterson." *The Brookings Review* (Fall): 18-23.

Buchholz, Rogene A. 1988. *Public Policy Issues for Management.* Englewood Cliffs, NJ: Prentice Hall.

Burns, James MacGregor. 1949. *Congress on Trial.* New York, NY: Harpers and Row.

_____. 1963. *The Deadlock of Democracy.* Englewood Cliffs, NJ: Prentice-Hall.

_____. 1984. *The Power To Lead: The Crisis of the American Presidency.* New York, NY: Simon and Schuster.

Business Week. 1990. "How To Get The Hill Humming Again." April 16, 1990, pp. 62, 63.

Chubb, John E. and Paul E. Peterson. 1989. *Can the Government Govern?* Washington, DC: The Brookings Institution.

Clark, Joseph. 1964. *Congress: The Sapless Branch.* New York, NY: Harper and Row.

_____, editor. 1965. *Congressional Reform: Problems and Prospects.* New York, NY: Thomas Y. Crowell.

Cleveland, Harlan. 1988. "Theses of a New Reformation: The Social Fallout of Science 300 Years After Newtown." *Public Administration Review* 48 (May/June): 681-686.

Cobb, Roger W. and Charles D. Elder. 1983. *Participation in American Politics: The Dynamics of Agenda-Building.* Baltimore, MD: Johns Hopkins University Press.

Congress and the Nation: A Review of Government and Politics. 1985. Volume VI, Washington, D.C.: Congressional Quarterly.

BIBLIOGRAPHY

Congressional Institute. ND. "Congressional Institute for the Future: Seeking Innovative Approaches to Emerging Policy Challenges." Washington, DC: Congressional Institute for the Future.

Cooper, Joseph. 1990. "Review of *The Transformation of the U.S. Senate* by Barbara Sinclair." *Political Science Quarterly* ___ (Fall): 488-489.

Cox, III, Raymond W. and Ralph P. Hummel. 1988. "A Congressional Declaration of Independence; Why Legislative Politics Cannot Be and Should Not Be Managed." Paper prepared for delivery at the Annual Meeting, American Political Science Association, Washington, D.C.

Crovitz, L. Gordon. 1990. "The Least Responsive Branch." *Commentary* ___ (March): 38-41.

Davidson, Roger H., David M. Kovenock and Michael K. O'Leary. 1966. *Congress in Crisis: Politics and Congressional Reform* Belmont, CA: Wadsworth Publishing Co.

Davidson, Roger H. and Walter J. Oleszek. 1977. *Congress Against Itself.* Bloomington, IN: Indiana University Press.

Davidson, Roger H. 1988. "Book Review of *Congress: Structure and Policy,* edited by Mathew D. McCubbins and Terry Sullivan." *American Political Science Review*, 82 (September): 1055-1057.

Dierkes, Meinolf, Hans N. Weiler and Ariane Berthoin Antal, editors. 1987. *Comparative Policy Research: Learning From Experience.* New York, NY: St. Martin's Press.

Dodd, Lawrence C. 1985. "Congress and the Quest for Power." *Studies in Congress.* Glenn R. Parker, editor. Washington, D.C.: Congressional Quarterly Press, 489-520.

Dodd, Lawrence C. and Bruce I. Oppenheimer, editors. 1985. *Congress Reconsidered.* Third edition. Washington, D.C.: Congressional Quarterly Press.

Donham, Philip and Robert J. Fahey. 1966. *Congress Needs Help.* New York, NY: Random House.

Dror, Yehezkel. 1986. *Policymaking Under Adversity.* New Brunswick, NJ: Transaction Books.

Dreyfus, Daniel A. 1976. "The Limitations of Policy Research in Congressional

Decision-Making." *Policy Studies Journal* 4 (Spring): 269-274.

Drucker, Peter. 1985. *Innovation and Entrepreneurship.* New York, NY: Harper and Row.

Economist. 1989. "Transport: Paved with Problems." *The Economist* (July 15, 1989): 23-24.

_____. 1991. "The British Constitution: A Modest Proposal." *The Economist* (July 6, 1991): 19-22.

Eidelberg, Paul. 1974. *A Discourse on Statesmanship: The Design and Transformation of the American Policy.* Urbana, IL: University of Illinois Press.

Elliott, William Yandell. 1935. *The Need for Constitutional Reform: A Program for National Security.* New York, NY: Whittlesey House, McGraw-Hill.

Ellwood, John W. 1985. "The Great Exception: The Congressional Budget Process in an Age of Decentralization," *Congress Reconsidered.* Lawrence C. Dodd and Bruce I. Oppenheimer, editors. Third edition. Washington, D.C.: Congressional Quarterly Press: 315-342.

―――. 1991. "Symposium Comment: On the new Politics of Public Policy." *Journal of Policy Analysis and Management* 10 (Summer): 426.433.

Elmore, Richard F. 1978. "Organizational Models of Social Program Implementation." *Public Policy* 26 (Spring): 185-228.

Etzioni, Amitai. 1967. "Mixed Scanning: A 'Third' Approach to Decision-Making." *Public Administration Review* 27 (December): 385-392.

―――. 1986. "Mixed Scanning Revisited." *Public Administration Review* 46 (January/February): 8-14.

―――. 1988. *The Moral Dimension: Toward a New Economics.* New York, NY: The Free Press.

―――. 1989. "Humble Decision Making." *Harvard Business Review* (July-August, 1989): 122-126.

Fenno, Jr., Richard F. 1975. "If, As Ralph Nader says, Congress is 'The Broken Branch,' How Come We Love Our Congressmen So Much?", in *Congress in Change: Evolution and Reform*, Norman J. Ornstein, editor. New York, NY: Praeger Publications: 277-287.

―――. 1988. "Congressional Research: Ideas for the Next Generation." *Extensions.* Carl Albert Congressional Research and Studies Center, University of Oklahoma. (Summer): 4-5.

Finletter, Thomas K. 1945. *Can Representative Government Do The Job?* New York, NY: Reynal and Hitchcock.

Fisher, Louis. 1981. *The Politics of Shared Power: Congress and the Executive.* Washington, D.C.: Congressional Quarterly Press.

Fisher, Roger and William Ury. 1983. *Getting to Yes: Negotiating Agreement Without Giving In.* New York, NY: Penguin Books.

Fiorina, Morris P. 1980. "The Decline of Collective Responsibility in American Politics." *Daedalus* 109 (Summer): 44.

Fogel, Richard L., Assistant Comptroller General. 1990. "How to Enhance Congressional Oversight: Statement before the Senate Committee on Banking, Subcommittee on HUD." Washington, DC: U.S. General Accounting Office, May 6, 1990.

Forester, John. 1984. "Bounded Rationality and the Politics of Muddling Through." *Public Administration Review*, Volume (January/February): 23-31.

Friedman, Milton. 1988. "Capitalism and Freedom." *Keeping The Tablets: Modern American Conservative Thought.* William F. Buckley, Jr., and Charles R. Keslar, editors. New York, NY: Harper and Row, 125-138.

Frye, Alton. 1976. "Congressional Politics and Policy Analysis: Bridging the Gap." *Policy Analysis* 2 (Spring): 265-281.

Garner, Les. 1988. "An Optimistic Case for Institutional Change." Paper presented to Annual Research Conference, Association for Public Policy Analysis and Management. Seattle, WA (October).

Goggin, Malcolm L. 1987. *Policy Design and the Politics of Implementation: The Case of Child Health Care in the American States.* Knoxville, TN: University of Tennessee Press.

―――; Bowman, Anne O'M.; Lester, James P.; and O'Toole, Jr., Laurence J. 1990. *Implementation Theory and Practice: Toward a Third Generation.* Glenview, IL: Scott Foresman.

Bibliography

Gortner, Harold F., Julianne Mahler and Jeanne Bell Nicholson. 1987. *Organization Theory: A Public Perspective*. Chicago, IL: Dorsey Press.

Graham, George. 1960. *America's Capacity to Govern: Some Preliminary Thoughts for Prospective Administrators*. University, AL: University of Alabama.

Green, Mark J., et al. 1979. *Who Runs Congress*. Third Edition, New York, NY: Viking.

Green, Mark and Mark Pinsky, editors. 1989. *America's Transition: Blueprints for the 1990's*. Democracy Project.

Gross, Bertram M. 1973. "Toward a House of Worse Repute or How to be a Rubber Stamp with Honor." *Committee Organization in the House*. U.S. Congress, House, Select Committee on Committees. 93rd Congress, 1st Session. Washington, D.C.: Government Printing Office: 767-783.

Gugliotta, Guy. 1991. "Reforming Congress by Committee." *Washington Post*, (August 1, 1991).

Guide to Congress. 1982. Third Edition. Washington, D.C.: Congressional Quarterly.

Hahn, Walter A. and Dennis L. Little, Editors. 1976. "Public Administration in the Third Century." *Public Administration Review* 36 (September/October): 577-613.

Hamilton, Edward K. 1978. "On Nonconstitutional Management of a Constitutional Problem." *Daedalus* 107 (Winter): 111-128.

Hanson, Royce. 1989. *The Minnesota Legislature and Its Leadership*. Minneapolis, MN: University of Minnesota Press.

Hardin, Charles M. 1974. *Presidential Power and Accountability: Toward a New Constitution*. Chicago, IL: University of Chicago Press.

Harmon, Michael M. and Richard T. Mayer. 1986. *Organization Theory for Public Administration*. Boston, MA: Little, Brown and Company.

Hayek, Frederick A. 1978. *New Studies in Philosophy, Politics, Economics and the History of Ideas*. Chicago, IL: University of Chicago Press.

Hazlitt, Henry. 1942. *A New Constitution Now*. New York, NY: Whittlesey House, McGraw-Hill.

Heatheryly, Charles L. and Burton Yale Pines, editors. 1989. *Mandate for Leadership III: Policy Struggles for the 1990s*. Washington, DC: Heritage Foundation.

Heclo, Hugh. 1978. "Issue Networks and the Executive Establishment." *The New American Political System*. Anthony King, editor. Washington, D.C.: American Enterprise Institute for Public Policy Research: 87-124.

Heineman, Robert A.; Bluhm, William T.; Peterson, Steven A.; and Kearney, Edward N. 1990. *The World of the Policy Analyst: Rationality, Values, and Politics*. Chatham, NJ: Chatham House Publishers.

Honadle, Beth Walter. 1986. "Defining and Doing Capacity Building: Perspectives and Experiences." *Perspectives on Management Capacity Building*. Beth Walter Honadle and Arnold M. Howitt, editors. Albany, NY: State University Press of New York Press. 9-23.

Honadle, Beth Walter, and Arnold M. Howitt, editors. 1986. *Perspectives on Management Capacity Building*. Albany, NY: State University Press of New York Press.

Huitt, Ralph K. 1965. "The Internal Distribution of Influence: The Senate." *The Congress and America's Future.* David Truman, editor. Englewood Cliffs, NJ: Prentice-Hall: 77-101.

Huntington, Samuel P. 1965. "Congressional Responses to the Twentieth Century." *The Congress and America's Future.* David Truman, editor. Englewood Cliffs, NJ: Prentice-Hall: 5-31.

Institute of Cultural Conservatism. 1988. *Cultural Conservatism: Toward A New National Agenda.* Free Congress Research and Education Foundation.

Jackall, Robert. 1988. *Moral Mazes: The World of Corporate Managers.* New York, NY: Oxford University Press.

Jacobs, Bruce and David Leo Weimer. 1986. "Inducing Capacity Building: The Role of the External Change Agent." *Perspectives on Management Capacity Building.* Beth Walter Honadle and Arnold M. Howitt, editors. Albany, NY: State University of New York Press: 139-160.

Jones, Charles O. 1975. "Somebody Must Be Trusted: An Essay on Leadership of the U.S. Congress." *Congress in Change: Evolution and Reform.* Norman J. Ornstein, editor. New York, NY: Praeger Publishers: 265-276.

_____. 1976. "Why Congress Can't Do Policy Analysis (or words to that effect)." 2 *Policy Analysis* (Spring): 251-264.

Jones, Gordon S. and John A. Marini, Editors. 1988. *The Imperial Congress: Crisis in the Separation of Powers.* New York, NY: Pharos Books.

Kanter, Rosabeth. 1983. *The Change Masters.* New York, NY: Simon and Schuster.

Kassebaum, Nancy Landon. 1988. "The Senate is Not in Order." *Washington Post.* January 27, 1988, A19.

Keller, Morton. 1988. "James Bryce and America." *Wilson Quarterly* 12 (Autumn): 92.

Kettl, Donald F. 1988. *Government by Proxy: (Mis)Managing Federal Programs.* Washington, D.C.: Congressional Quarterly Press.

Kingdon, John W. 1973. *Congressmen's Voting Decisions.* New York, NY: Harper and Row.

_____. 1984. *Agendas, Alternatives and Public Policies.* Boston, MA: Little, Brown and Company.

Kornacki, John J., Editor. 1990. *Leading Congress: New Styles, New Strategies.* Washington, DC: CQ Press.

Korten, David C. 1981. "The Management of Social Transformation." *Public Administration Review* 41 (November/December): 609-618.

Laad, Everett Carll. 1990. "Public Opinion and the 'Congress' Problem." *The Public Interest* 100 (Summer): 57-67.

Lauth, Thomas P. 1985. "Performance Evaluation in the Georgia Budgetary Process. *Public Budgeting and Finance* ___ (Spring): 67-82.

Leach, James and William P. McKenzie, editors. 1989. *A Newer World: The Progressive Republican Vision of America.* Lanham, MD: Madison Books, University Press of America.

Levin, Martin A. and Barbara Ferman. 1985. *The Political Hand: Policy Implementation and Youth Employment Programs.* New York, NY: Pergamon Press.

Lindblom, Charles E. 1959. "The Science of 'Muddling Through'" *Public Administration Review* 19 (Spring): 79-88.

_____. 1979. "Still Muddling, Not Yet Through." *Public Administration Review* 39 (November/December): 517-525.

Linden, Russell M. 1990. *From Vision to Reality: Strategies of Successful Innovators in Government.* Charlottesville, VA: LEL Enterprises.

Lipset, Seymour Martin and William Schneider. 1983. *The Confidence Gap.* New York, NY: Free Press.

Lowi, Theodore J., editor. 1965. *Legislative Politics U.S.A.* Second edition. Boston, MA: Little, Brown, and Company.

Maass, Arthur. 1983. *Congress and the Common Good.* New York, NY: Basic Books.

MacDonald, William. 1921. *A New Constitution for America.* New York, NY: B.W. Huebsch.

MacRae, Jr., Duncan. 1985. *Policy Indicators: Links Between Social Science and Public Debate.* Chapel Hill, NC: University of North Carolina Press.

Matthews, Donald R. and James A. Stimson. 1975. *Yeas and Nays: Normal Decision Making in the U.S. House of Representatives.* New York, NY: John Wiley and Sons.

Mazmanian, Daniel A. and Paul A. Sabatier. 1983. *Implementation and Public Policy.* Glenview, IL: Scott, Foresman and Company.

McCubbins, Matthew D. and Thomas Schwartz. 1984. "Congressional Oversight Overlooked: Policy Patrols versus Fire Alarms." *American Journal of Political Science* 28 (February): 165-179.

Meehan, Eugene J. 1990. *Ethics for Policymaking: A Methodological Analysis.* New York, NY: Greenwood Press.

Melloan, Goerge. 1989. "Doing Badly Trying to Do Good on Capitol Hill." *Wall Street Journal* (July 18, 1989): A15.

Melnick, R. Shep. 1991. "Introduction to Symposium on the New Politics of Public Policy." *Journal of Policy Analysis and Management* 10 (Summer): 363-368.

Mezey, Michael L. 1989. *Congress, the President and Public Policy.* Boulder, CO: Westview Press.

Morgan, Gareth. 1986. *Images of Organization.* Beverly Hills, CA: Sage Publications.

Morrill, Calvin. 1988. *Moral Mazes: The World of Corporate Managers.* New York, NY: Oxford University Press.

Murray, Charles. 1988. *In Pursuit of Happiness and Good Government.* New York, NY: Simon and Schuster.

Nagel, Stuart S. and Marian Neef. 1979. *Policy Analysis in Social Science Research.* Beverly Hills, CA: Sage Publications.

Nagel, Stuart S. 1988. *Policy Studies: Integration and Evaluation.* New York, NY: Praeger.

Ogul, Morris S. 1976. *Congress Oversees the Bureaucracy: Studies in Legislative Supervision.* Pittsburgh, PA: University of Pittsburgh Press.

Oleszek, Walter J. 1984. *Congressional Procedures and the Policy Process.* Second edition. Washington, D.C.: Congressional Quarterly Press.

Oppenheimer, Bruce I. 1985. "Changing Time Constraints on Congress: Historical Perspectives on the Use of Cloture." *Congress Reconsidered*. Lawrence C. Dodd and Bruce I. Oppenheimer, editors. Third edition. Washington, D.C.: Congressional Quarterly Press: 393-413.

Ornstein, Norman J., Editor. 1975. *Congress in Change: Evolution and Reform*. New York, NY: Praeger Publishers.

_____. 1984. *Vital Statistics on Congress, 1945-1985 Edition*. Washington, D.C.: American Enterprise Institute.

_____. 1990. "The Permanent Democratic Congress." *The Public Interest* 100 (Summer): 24-44.

_____. 1990. "Can Congress Be Led?" *Leading Congress: New Styles, New Strategies*. John J. Kornacki, Editor. Washington, DC: CQ Press: 13-25.

_____, Robert L. Peabody, and David W. Rhode. 1985. "The Senate Through The 1980's: Cycles of Change." *Congress Reconsidered*. Lawrence C. Dodd and Bruce I. Oppenheimer, editors. Third edition. Washington, D.C.: Congressional Quarterly Press: 13-33.

Parker, Glenn R., editor. 1985. *Studies of Congress*. Washington, D.C.: Congressional Quarterly Press.

Patterson, Samuel C. 1978. "The Semi-Sovereign Congress." *The New American Political System*. Anthony King, editor. Washington, D.C.: American Enterprise Institute: 125-177.

Pearson, Drew and Jack Anderson. 1968. *The Case Against Congress*. New York, NY: Simon and Schuster.

Polsby, Nelson W., editor. 1971. *Congressional Behavior*. New York, NY: Random House.

_____. 1975. "Legislatures." *Handbook of Political Science*. Fred Greenstein, et al., editors. Reading, MA: Addison-Wesley: 257-319.

_____. 1984. *Political Innovation in America: The Politics of Policy Initiation* New Haven, CT: Yale University Press.

_____. 1986. *Congress and the Presidency*. Fourth edition. Englewood Cliffs, NJ: Prentice-Hall.

_____. 1990. "Congress-Bashing for Beginners." *The Public Interest* 100 (Summer): 15-23.

Popper, Karl. "The Open Society and Its Enemies Revisited." *The Economist*. April 23, 1988: 19-22.

Pops, Gerald M. and Max O. Stephenson, Jr. 1987. *Conflict Resolution in the Policy Process*. Morgantown, WV: Department of Public Administration, West Virginia University.

President's Commission on National Goals. *Goals for Americans: Programs for Action in the Sixties*. New York, NY: Spectrum Books, Prentice-Hall.

Pressman Jeffrey and Aaron Wildavsky. 1984. *Implementation*. Third edition. Berkeley, CA: University of California Press.

Price, David E. 1985. "Congressional Committees in the Policy Process." *Congress Reconsidered*. Lawrence C. Dodd and Bruce I. Oppenheimer, editors. Third edition. Washington, D.C.: Congressional Quarterly Press: 161-188.

BIBLIOGRAPHY

Price, Don K. 1983. *America's Unwritten Constitution: Science, Religion and PoliticalResponsibility.* Baton Rouge, LA: Louisiana State University Press.

Quinn, James Brian. 1989. "Strategic Change: 'Logical Incrementalism.'" *Sloan Management Review* (Summer): 45-60.

Quinn, Robert E. *Beyond Rational Management: Mastering the Paradoxes and Competing Demands of High Performance.* San Francisco, CA: Jossey-Bass.

Ranney, Austin. 1976. "The Divine Science: Political Engineering in American Culture." *American Political Science Review* 70 (March): 140-148.

Rapaport, Daniel. 1975. *Inside the House.* Chicago, IL: Follett Publishing Company.

Riddick, Floyd M. 1949. *The United States Congress Organization and Procedure.* Manassas, VA: National Capitol Publishers, Inc.

Rieselbach, Leroy N. 1973. *Congressional Politics.* New York, NY: McGraw-Hill.

_____. 1977. *Congressional Reform in the Seventies.* Morristown, NJ: General Learning Press.

_____. 1978. *Legislative Reform: The Policy Impact.* Lexington, MA: Lexington Books.

Riker, William H. 1988. *Liberalism Against Populism: A Confrontation Between the Theory of Democracy and the Theory of Social Choice.* Prospect Heights, IL: Waveland Press.

Ripley, Randall B. 1983. *Congress: Process and Policy.* Third edition. New York, NY: Norton.

_____ and Grace A. Franklin. 1987. *Congress, the Bureaucracy and Public Policy.* Fourth edition. Chicago, IL: Dorsey Press.

_____. 1991. *Congress, The Bureaucracy, and Public Policy.* Fifth edition. Pacific Grove, CA: Brooks/Cole.

Rittel, Horst W.J. and Melvin Webber. 1973. "Dilemmas in a General Theory of Planning." *Policy Sciences* 4 (June): 160.

Rivlin, Alice M. 1987. "Economics and the Political Process." *American Economic Review* 77 (March): 1-10.

Robinson, Donald L. 1987. *To the Best of My Ability: The Presidency and the Constitution.* New York, NY: Norton.

_____ 1989. *Government for the Third American Century.* Boulder, CO: Westview Press.

Rodale, Robert. 1988. "Big New Ideas—Where Are They Today?" *Technological Literacy.* Arlington, Virginia: Third National Science, Technology and Society Conference, February 5-7, 1988.

Sagoff, Mark. 1988. *The Economy of the Earth: Philosophy, Law and the Environment.* New York, NY: Cambridge University Press.

Sawhill, Isabel V., Editor. 1988. *Challenge to Leadership: Economic and Social Issues for the Next Decade.* Washington, DC: Urban Institute.

Scher, Seymour. 1963. "Conditions for Legislative Control." *Journal of Politics* 25 (August): 526-551.

Schick, Allen. 1976. "The Supply and Demand for Analysis on Capitol Hill." 2 *Policy Analysis* (Spring): 215-234.

_____ and Harry Hatry. 1982. "Zero-Base Budgeting: The Manager;s Budget." *Public Budgeting and Finance* ___ (Winter: 72-87.

Schubert, Glendon A. 1960. *The Public Interest.* New York, NY: The Free Press.

Scruton, Roger. 1982. *A Dictionary of Political Thought.* New York: Harper and Row.

Shepsle, Kenneth A. 1988. "Representation and Governance: The Great Legislative Trade-Off." *Political Science Quarterly* 103 (Fall): 461-484.

Simms, Margaret C., editor. 1989. *Black Economic Progress: An Agenda for the 1990s.* Joint Center for Political Studies.

Simon, Herbert A. 1945. *Administrative Behavior: A Study of Decision-Making Process in Administrative Organization.* New York, NY: MacMillan.

Sinclair, Barbara. 1985. "Agenda, Policy and Alignment Change from Coolidge to Reagan." *Congress Reconsidered.* Lawrence C. Dodd and Bruce I. Oppenheimer, editors. Third edition. Washington, D.C.: Congressional Quarterly Press: 291-314.

Smith, Steven S. 1989. *Call to Order: Floor Politics in the House and Senate.* Washington, DC: The Brookings Institution.

Smith, Steven S. and Christopher J. Deering. 1984. *Committees in Congress.* Washington, D.C.: Congressional Quarterly Press.

Smith, T. Alexander. 1988. *Time and Public Policy.* Knoxville, TN: University of Tennesse Press.

Smithies, Arthur. 1955. *The Budgetary Process.* New York, NY: McGraw-Hill.

Stein, Herbert. 1989. "Problems and No-Problems of the American Economy." *The AEI Economist* (June, 1989): 1-8.

Steinbruner, John D. 1974. *The Cybernetic Theory of Decision.* Princeton, NJ: Princeton University Press.

Steinbruner, Maureen, editor. 1989. *American Tomorrow: The Choices We Face, A Report of the Governance Project.* Washington, DC: Center for National Policy Press.

Stephenson, Max O., Jr. and Gerald M. Pops. 1989. "Conflict Resolution Methods and the Policy Process." *Public Administration Review* 49 (September/October): 463-473.

Stillman, II, Richard J. 1988. "The Future of the American Constitution and the Administrative State After the Bicentennial: Some Reflections." *Public Administration Review* 48 (July/August): 813-815.

Stone, Clarence N. 1985. "Efficiency versus Social Learning: A Reconsideration of the Implementation Process." *Policy Studies Review* 4 (February): 484-496.

Sundquist, James L. 1980. "The Crisis of Competence in Our National Government." *Political Science Quarterly* 95 (Summer): 183-208.

_____. 1981. *The Decline and Resurgence of Congress.* Washington, D.C.: The Brookings Institution.

_____. 1986. *Constitutional Reform and Effective Government.* Washington, D.C.: The Brookings Institution.

Swiss, James E. 1991. *Public Management Systems: Monitoring and Managing Government Performance.* Englewood Cliffs, NJ: Prentice-Hall.

Bibliography

Thompson, Fred. 1989. "Due Process: Broadening and Gutting the Administrative State." *Public Administration Review* (September/October): 492-494.

Time. October 23, 1989. "Is Government Dead?" 34 (Number 18): 28-34.

Toft, Graham S. 1986. "Building Capacity to Govern." *Perspectives on Management Capacity Building.* Beth Walter Honadle and Arnold M. Howitt, editors. Albany, New York: State University of New York Press: pp. 242-267.

Toulmin, Stephen. 1988. "The Recovery of Practical Philosophy." *The American Scholar* 56 (Summer): 337-352.

Truman, David B. 1959. *The Congressional Party: A Case Study.* New York, NY: John Wiley & Sons.

_____. 1965. "Introduction: The Problem in Its Setting." *The Congress and America's Future,* David Truman, editor. Englewood Cliffs, NJ: Prentice-Hall: 1-4.

Tugwell, Rexford G. 1970. *A Model Constitution for a United Republics of America.* Santa Barbara, CA: Center for the Study of Democratic Institutions.

_____. 1974. *The Emerging Constitution.* New York, NY: Harper's Magazine Press.

_____. 1976. *The Compromising of the Constitution: Early Departures.* Notre Dame, IN: University of Notre Dame Press.

U.S. Congress, Joint Economic Committee, House Committee on Small Business and Congressional Clearinghouse on the Future. 1984. *The New Economy: Proceedings of a Congressional Economic Conference.* Washington, DC: U.S. Government Printing Office.

U.S. General Accounting Office, Comptroller General. 1977. *Finding Out How Programs are Working: Suggestions for Congressional Oversight.* Washington, D.C.: Government Printing Office.

U.S. House of Representatives, Committee on Rules. 1980. *Sunset, Sunrise and Related Measures.* Washington, D.C.: Government Printing Office.

U.S. Senate, Committee on Government Operations, Subcommittee on Oversight Procedures. 1976. *Legislative Oversight and Program Evaluation.* Washington, D.C.: U.S. Government Printing Office.

Uslaner, Eric M. 1990. "Review of '*Congress, the President, and Public Policy*' by Michael L. Mezey." *Political Science Quarterly* ___ (Fall): 492-494.

Vogler, David J. and Sidney R. Waldman. 1985. *Congress and Democracy.* Washington, D.C.: Congressional Quarterly, Inc.

Weaver, Jr., Warren. 1972. *Both Your Houses.* New York, NY: Praeger.

Webber, David J. 1984. "Political Conditions Motivating Legislator's Use of Policy Information." *Policy Studies Review,* August 1984, Volume 4, No. 1, pp. 110-118.

Willard, Timothy and Daniel M. Fields. 1989. "Helping Congress Look Ahead." *The Futurist* (May-June): 23-27.

Williams, David G., Max O. Stephenson, Jr., and David J. Webber. 1991. "Teaching the Missing Pieces of Policy Analysis." *PS: Political Science and Politics* 24 (June): 218-220.

Wilson, H.H. 1951. *Congress: Corruption and Compromise.* New York, NY: Holt.

Wilson, James Q. 1966. "Innovation in Organization: Notes Toward a Theory." *Approaches to Organizational Design*. James D. Thompson, editor. Pittsburgh, PA: University of Pittsburgh Press: 193-223.

Wilson, Woodrow. 1885. *Congressional Government: A Study in American Politics*. Introduction by Walter Lippman, originally published in 1885. Gloucester, MA: Peter Smith, 1973.

Wright, Gerald C., Leroy N. Rieselbach and Lawrence C. Dodd. 1986. *Congress and Policy Change*. New York, NY: Agathon Press.

Zwirn, Jerrold. 1983. *Congressional Publications: A Guide to Legislation, Budgets and Treaties*. Littleton, CO: Libraries Unlimited, Inc.

INVITATION TO NETWORK

The Interactivity Foundation and the author are very interested in your comments and responses to the Plenary Review concept. We are interested in your assessment–whether positive or negative–as well as your suggestions. Your response will help in the further development and application of Plenary Review.

Please mail your comments/responses to either address:

Dr. David Williams, Chair and Professor
Department of Public Administration
302 Woodburn Hall
West Virginia University
Morgantown, WV 26506

Interactivity Foundation
Post Office Box 8
Parkersburg, WV 26102-0008